A TEENAGER'S WAR
(a sixteen year old boy's memory of the Civil War)

Written by George Richardson Cruzen
Glenda Jensen (Great-great granddaughter)

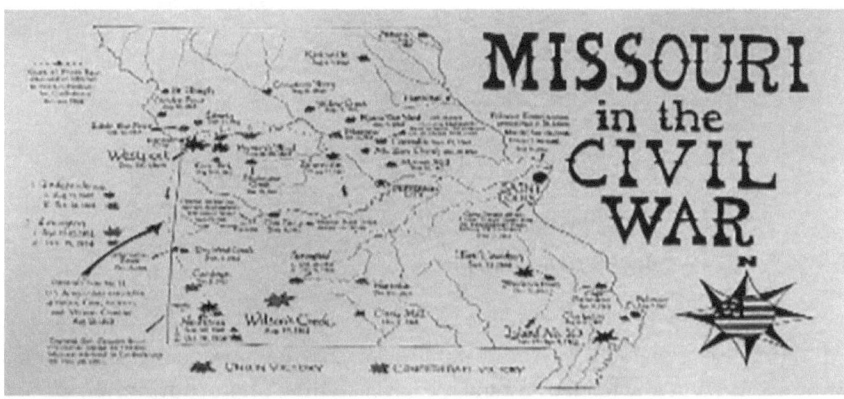

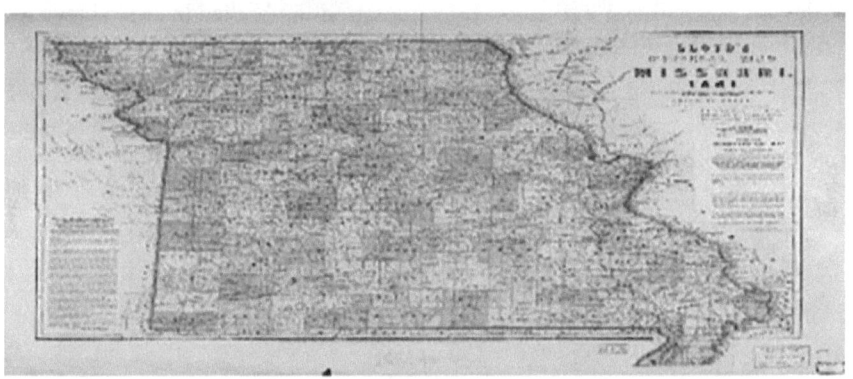

The recollection of a sixteen-year-old boy
concerning the Civil War and his involvement

BookSide Press
877-741-8091
www.booksidepress.com
orders@booksidepress.com

FOREWORD

As we take a few years to step back into time, I did some research about this war and perhaps learned something that was not in the history books when I was in school. I learned that even though the commanders in charge actually had beards including President Abraham Lincoln. Even Robert E. Lee had a beard. However, many of the young men who served in the armies both North and South did not sport any kind of facial hair. Why? The majority of the soldiers were teenagers – too young to shave.

The story is so straight forward and was written by someone who actually was there. His recollections are personal and from the viewpoint of a teenage boy. This is a nonpolitical story as well as nonracist. It's just a simple story told by a teenage boy who was born at Harper's Ferry, Virginia with the family moving to Miami, Missouri.

There are actual stories which told what he observed and some funny stories that will make readers laugh. This is a story for complete enjoyment.

Now I'm ready to introduce to you my great- great grandfather, George Richardson "Dick" Cruzen.

GENEALOGICAL INFORMATION GEORGE RICHARDSON CRUZEN

George Richardson Cruzen was with Quantrill. A veteran of 22 battles in the Civil War, Cruzen was described as slight of stature, clear blue eyes. He was born at Harpers Ferry, VA and when he was young moved with his parents and siblings to Saline County in Missouri where they settled 16 miles north of Marshall. When the war broke out Cruzen was for the North but switched to the South when Federal troops fired on women and children in St. Louis. He was sixteen at the time and was attending the Miami Male Institute. The school was dismissed because most of the students were joining the military – both sides. His father refused to permit him to join any military group, so he went to work on the farm. When the Union Calvary were marching south from Laciede and pillaging the country, he joined 150 men who volunteered to drive back the Federals.

Cruzen was captured and kept prisoner for several months at Laclede. He took the oath not to bear arms against the Union and was released. Shortly after his return to the farm, he was impressed into the Union Militia at Miami, Missouri, then a river town of a population of 1200. He declined a 2nd Lieutenancy. Through a young woman, he met three of Quantrill's men hiding in the hills near Miami. They were doing recruiting work. He returned to the Union camp for his clothes when he was stopped by his captain. He told the captain that he was riding out of town to look for Mrs. Zooks's cow, which had strayed. It was the cow that furnished milk for the troops. So, the captain told him to proceed. Cruzen was betrayed by the young woman and nearly killed from an ambush. Be he succeeded in joining Quintrill's forces in Jackson County, Missouri.

The Quantrill men rode south to Texas where Cruzen left the guerrillas to join the brigade of General Shelby. Cruzen was a bugler and served as Colonel B. F. Gordon's orderly. When the regimental adjutant was killed near Jefferson City, Colonel Gordon placed the duties of the adjutant upon the shoulders of Cruzen. He was only 18 when he fought at the Battle of Westport as he joined Quantrill on July 20, 1863. He attended the Quantrill reunions after the war. At various times, after the war, he lived in Kansas City and in Independence Missouri. George died June 8, 1936 in Jefferson City. He was buried in Warrensburg, Missouri.

(freepages.genealogy.rootsweb.ancestry.com/jrbakerjr/Missouri/ georgecruzen.htm)

SHOUT OUTS

1. I want to thank my great-great grandpa in heaven for this story.

2. I want to thank my grandmother, Mary Mildred Delaplain Jensen for giving me this story.

3. I wish to thank my family for encouraging my writing.

4. But mostly I wish to thank my Lord God for giving me the gift of writing.

Men and Commanding Officers who served alongside of George Richardson "Dick" Cruzen;

Brothers	Men	Commanding Officers
Nathanial "Nat" Cruzen	Thomas Winning	Captain Balew
I. C. "Ikie"	Joe Hall	Captain Arch Burnsides
	John Burnsides	Captain Grand Burnsides
	Barney Mayfield	Lt. Dickey
	Andy Campbell	Gen. Col. Shelby
	Frank Robinson	Captain Green
	Jim Elson	General Holmes
	John Snelling	Lt. Bob Thompson
	Ward Stonehouse	Col. Gordon
	Jim Elson	General Steele
	Joe Pitman	General Fagan
	Steve Harris	Lt. Flener
	John Steele	Sgt. Thomas Ingram
	Ryal Crower	Col. Shanks
	George McQue	Col. Blackwell
	Ike Ulrey	Capt. Red
	Wallace Elder	Col. Dobins
	Rile Crawdue	Lt. Lankford
	Bill Bledsaw	General Price
	Thomas Ingram	Lt. Perry Catron
	Dave Ferril	Capt. Chrispin
	Ike Shelby	Capt. Moreman
	Will Pierce	Lt. John Flenner

Glenda Jensen

	Mark Morgan	Major Gordon
	Sam Hildebrande	Major Cravens
	Al Jeffries	Captain Elliott
	A. McCoy	Col. Slawback
	Dave Pagle	
	Harry Hammer	
	Dave Paine	

A TEENAGER'S WAR
(a sixteen-year-old boy's memory of the Civil War)
Written by George Richardson Cruzen
Biography by Glenda Jensen (great- great granddaughter)

BEFORE THE WAR

I was born in Harper's Ferry, Virginia on November 30th, 1844 and came to Missouri in Spring of 1849. However, I remember very little of Harper's Ferry or the trip to Missouri. One thing that I do remember while being four was the time that my brother, I.C. also known as Ike and my sister, Eliza, were lined up in the front room of his house to be baptized by a Methodist preacher.

The preacher commenced with my brother I. C. (Ikie) with a bowl of water in his hand and dipped other hand in it and put the water on I. C.'s head. In the meantime, I broke from the other end of the line and ran into the hall and down the steps to the basement and outdoors. My sister, Margaret, caught me and brought me back crying and said, "tell that preacher to go home and wash his own children's faces. That was probably the incident that kept me from joining the Methodist Church.

I barely remember the trip to Missouri. We left Harper's Ferry early in March on the B. and O. (Baltimore and Ohio) Railroad. At the end of the railroad up in the mountains, we took a stagecoach to Wheeling, West Virginia. After that, we took a steamboat to Cincinnati and changed to a larger boat. While we were there, my father bought some furniture. I remember the old cook stove so well as my mother used it 'til I was near grown.

From there we traveled to St. Louis, where we changed boats for Miami, Missouri where we landed in April. I also remember very little of that trip as well. One thing I do remember is that on one of boats we had frogs' legs for dinner. I. C., my brother, wanted more. I guess he really liked them. The waiter told us that it was fried chicken. My brother asked, "why can't we have some of the other parts of the chicken besides legs?" The waiter simply said, "other people who ate first had eaten all of the other parts except for the legs." Well, who were we to complain? The legs were delicious. Soon after dinner, one of our older sisters told us that it was frogs' legs. We all got mad because they fed us frogs. Oh well, they were good anyway.

Meanwhile, my older brother, Nathanial (Nat) had come to Missouri the year before. He and another man met us a Miami with two ox wagons. They loaded the furniture in the wagons and put us children on top and started to the farm which was five mile east. I remember as we came in sight of our future home, we came into a little prairie east of the place. My sister, Margaret, and I were walking in front of the first wagon when she declared, "Dick, there is our home!" I remarked, "Well it is a little house for all of us". She said, "Father has plans to build more to it before we go there. We are going on to a neighbor's house 'til he gets it built." Keep in mind that it was only one room with an attic, and there were nine children at that time.

It was about sundown at that time, and as we were traveling through the woods, I heard a Whippoorwill near us. I asked, "What in the world is that?" My sister saw an opportunity to come up with this answer, "It says 'whip you well.'" She had me laughing 'til my sides ached. Then I asked if I could get on top the wagon as I was getting tired of walking. The wagon stopped, and I had to be lifted up onto the wagon. We finally reached the neighbor's house about dark and stayed there until Father built another log room. Our house ended up being two stories including the attic being transformed into a room as well. It was only a week before we moved into our new home.

In the spring of 1850, my brother, Nat, along with several others went to California in an ox wagon. I remember that I went with him to Brunswick for supplies. He had two yoke oxen to the wagon while we got the supplies across the river. Some guns were in the lot as I remember, and while we were going home, we had to cross swamps in the bottom where the water came up to the wagon box (the body of a wagon). Shoot! The river was about overflowing.

In May of 1850, my brother I. C. was driving two yoke of oxen while a black woman was hold the plow. The ground had been broken the year before so there were big bunches of grass in places where Father was planting corn near them. I had platted hemp crackers for I. C.'s whip and took it to him. They were about ¼ mile south of the house when I finally handed them over. He asked, "Dick, what's wrong with your foot?" I looked down and saw that my right foot was bleeding. I had not noticed it before, but something seemed to tell me what to say. I quietly said that a snake bit it. He exclaimed, "What kind of snake?" I said, "a rattle snake." He asked, "Where is it". I pointed over to a big bunch of grass. I. C. quickly told my father, and he went to the place and found the snake and killed it. It had three rattlers. So, he carried me most of the way home. I did run part of the way.

Father cut the places with his pocket knife, so they bled freer and used whites of eggs and allum to draw out the poison. He sent for a doctor, but when the doctor arrived, he proudly proclaimed that my father had done a good job. He did want me to drink some whiskey, so I wouldn't feel the pain. I quickly said, "NO!" It was a close call for me as my leg swelled up to the thigh, but I soon got over it. I remember that Dr. Dunlap had a big wad of tobacco in his mouth and made one cheek look larger than the other, so I called him the lopsided faced doctor. After that incident, I had always thought that there was a Superior force which told me what to tell I. C. (Ikie).

In September 1850, I with some of my sisters and my brother, I. C., started to school at the school house about 2 ¼ miles east (tick district). It was named this because of the innumerable number of them around the school. It was a log house with a big fireplace that it took a large log of wood. It was built of logs and lined with rock and mud. The seats were split logs with peg legs of wood. No back rest. I only went two months. In 1851 Father and some neighbors built a log schoolhouse ½ mile west of our home. It also had split log seats but a stove for heart.

I went to that school for three years and four months. Each year after that, the district was divided, and I went to the Bluff School. It was a good frame 2 ½ miles west. I went there for four months as well. After that we went for eight months of school. Miss Jane Lent was teacher for five months during the fall and winter and three months of summer. In the summer or spring term, I was the oldest boy. I finished Grammar, Arithmetic, and Ancient History. In September, I started to the Miami Male Institute. [1] [2]

THE WAR BEGINS

I rode a horse from home five miles and never missed a day during the school year. I also started there again in 1860 and stopped in May 1861 when the war started in Missouri.

When I was not in school, I worked on the farm. When I became 10 years old, I bought a gun and soon got to be a good hunter for a boy. Soon after I bought the gun, I went squirrel hunting alone down the branch north of our home. About a mile down the branch and while up on a bluff, I saw something in a tree about 50 feet from me. Just a little above me, the big ears and eyes and big head made me think it was a wild cat I had seen dead once. I had only a squirrel load in my gun but decided to shoot it. Then as it fell, I saw that it was an owl, but I sure felt scared when I saw it first.

---

1   incorporated on 3-12-1859
2   Similar Name: Miami Academy

When I entered the Miami Male Institute under Professor J. H. Yonley, my father put me under his direction as he saw best. He also told me that I needed to study hard. When I would do that, the Professor would put me back in Algebra. However, I was put in the second part of Algebra as opposed to the other chaps. Because of this, I was a year ahead of everyone else.

In the M. M. I., there were a lot of boys aged 19 – 21 and some were for session; there were lots of arguments. As I recall, it was about the 13th or 14th of May when our school dismissed about 3 pm. We heard a lot of shouts and yelling downtown. I rode there to see what it was about, and I found T. T. Bell, our State Senator, on a good's box telling about what had happened, and in his closing words he said it is war forced on us by the government at Washington.

I got the St. Louis Christian Advocate and Republican and took it home the next day. I took my books home, quit school, and was a Southerner afterwards. An article in the paper claimed that there were some women, old men, and children killed by Brenstein's 54th Massachusetts Regiment. [3]

My brother, I. C. (Isaac Chaplain), enlisted in Crews Calvary Company a few days after this happened and went with them to Lexington then went south with a company of infantry which soon left Miami. I stayed on the farm and worked. In September we heard the cannons booming at Lexington. A few days after I was standing on our front porch and saw Ikie, my brother, ride up. Father and I ran to him and lifted him off his horse and carried him to the house. He said that he was very sick.

Father soon found out that he had Pneumonia and began to doctor him. He had rode from Lexington to home all the while being sick. He was in bed for nearly a month. One night soon after

---

3   The 54th Massachusetts Infantry Regiment was an infantry regiment that saw extensive service in the Union Army during the American Civil War. The unit organized in the northern states during the Civil War. Wikipedia
Active: March 13, 1863 – August 4, 1865
Size: 1,100 members

he began to improve, an old school friend older than me, Robinson Kile who had moved to Carroll County, came to visit. I went to the door with my father. He said that the Federals had come down from Laclede and were taking all the bacon, flour, and all the cattle fit for beef they can get. So, Robinson and I decided to meet in Miami to drive them back. Thomas Winning, who moved in with Father, and I went together to Miami.

However only 20 of us crossed the river and joined up with Logan Balew. We had about 150 men at that time. Then they all went North and during the night, it rained hard most of the way and then quite cool in the morning. As a result, Thomas Winning had a chill and turned back home.

The rest went on North to Big Herican Creek, and Balew lined us up and told us that there were 300 Federals along with two pieces of artillery. So, we would go to the crossing and wait for them, but a lot of them said we can't fight 300. So those with good arms and cannon sense began to ride away.

I remember that Captain Balew was a few feet of me, and I said, "Captain, just call for all that will go with you and give them a round at least (remember I was only 16)." He said, "young man, you are right." So, he called out for all that would to follow him. Fifty of us went, and it was the first Bushwhack [4] in the state. Captain Balew placed me behind a big stump. I had a good deer rifle and a single barrel pistol, but I had to get both wet; neither fired. I sat there, took a pin, and opened the wet powder in the tubes of gun pistol packed dry powder in and put on dry caps, but the fight was over. We then hurried to our horses. I never knew if any were killed, but a lot were wounded when they fired their cannons 'til we were several miles away, and Balew ordered us to go home.

We had heard more were coming from Miami early that morning, so we were expecting to meet them.

---

4   a surprise attack

About two miles west of Dewit, the boys in front rode down a path across a creek to take a short cut to Miami. There was a limb of a tree bending over so much that we had to duck down. Joe Hall, a former school friend from Dewit, was behind me. I said, "Joe, duck low!" He had a short britch loading gun that he took off a wounded Federal, and he caught it about the mussel. The limb caught the hammer, and it shot him between the thumb and finger of his left hand. I stopped and took my handkerchief and bound it. Then we started on to catch the others, but we saw several going towards Dewit and calling out. We first thought that they were from Miami and stopped. When we got closer, we discovered that one person was wearing a blue uniform.

My first thought was to shoot him, but I brought my gun off my shoulder. I feared that it may not fire correctly, so we surrendered. There were a few Federals and some recruits let Joe go to Dewit in order to get his hand dressed. However, he went to the river and then waded on across. The same men, who had captured Thomas Winning, heard a canon and then decided to let him go the next morning but kept his gun.

They took me and several others they had captured to the command on Big Herican where we had fought and then sent us to Laclede [5]. They tied our hands behind our backs and made us walk even though they had two wagons with six or eight wounded. However, they did let us get into the wagons in order to cross the Grand River. It just so happened that John Burnsides whom I had gone to school with had begged the Lieutenant to let me ride since I dressed his wounded leg as we continued our travels. When we arrived at Laclede, we were put in a boxed-up wood house with no blankets, but Barney Mayfield, an old friend, loaned me his so I did not have to suffer.

The next morning Old Mr. Gilbert, a friend of my Father, came to me and said, "George, I am going to get you out of this; be careful what you say if you have told a lie, stick to it because they can't prove it."

---

5   Laclede, Missouri – just north of Kansas City, MO

I was kept there nearly two weeks but was treated well as I had friends there then, Thomas Winning and Andy Campbell. Then a strange Union man came to help get me out, and Father sent word to me to take the others and come home. I could not expect to be exchanged as I had not been enlisted as a soldier but I was to bring the others and come home anyway. It was late October 1861.

My brother, I. C. was then convalescing at home when I got there. Within a week or two, our house was burned and most everything we owned had burned as well.

I. C. and I had been sleeping, but it was not a good sleep. Suddenly I turned toward the window and saw a light. I raised up and could see the blaze. I called Father and hollered at him to let him know that the house or something was on fire. I grabbed some of my clothes and took boots in one hand and ran to the front door. I got out with a full suit, the only one that was able to do just that. We found out that it was a cabin burning. Father and I ran to the door and broke it in just in time to save Unle Yourk. By this time the smoke house was burning as well as the kitchen.

A Union man and friend told Father that he was in Brunswick and heard about it being planned, but our dogs just kept sleeping on the porch. They had set the log cabin on fire instead of the house. Father was told that it was a neighbor but promised him not tell.

In December 1861 Frank Robinson recruited a regiment of infantry in Miami. Ikie was not well enough to go, so my brother, Nat, went instead. Ikie stayed with Nat's wife. However, they were captured at Blackwater and taken to St Louis then afterward to Alton. I stayed at home and planted a crop for Father in the Spring of 1862 as well as in the Spring of 1863. But in May of 1863 Uncle York and I were plowing corn, and three armed men were waiting at the end of the row. They told me, "We have come for you, George, with orders to put you in the militia. So, you must go with us to Grand Burnsides." I tried to beg off but soon saw that it was no use. Father came and tried and then said, "You have no horse or saddle." They had kept my horse and all I had when I was captured. Finally, I said, "Father, if I had a good saddle, I would ride that three-year-old bay colt; he is a good one." Jim Elson, who was in charge of the squad, told me that I could have his saddle and that he could get another one when he gets home. So, we caught the colt, saddled him up, and I got on. Jim led him 'til I got him so I could guide him.

I was taken to Arrow Rock where the company was organized. Old Captain Arch Burnsides was appointed to organize it. Grant Burnsides was elected Captain and then the first lieutenant then the second lieutenant. There was three voted for positions. Furgeson got 17 votes, then 10 and then 16. All the Southern men voted for me. Capt. Burnsides came to me and told me to withdraw. It wouldn't do me good to run because I didn't want to be in this regiment. I told him that my loyalty was with the South. I was hoping to be released from this service.

In June we were ordered to Lexington and as we went through Marshall, we got a bugle, and I was the only one that could blow it. So, I gave up my gun for the bugle. We were in Lexington until August then off to Miami, and Capt. Burnsides and about 8 or 10 of us got a widow to take our stations and cook for us. Mrs. Miller and her daughters were neighbors, so I went there frequently and met Miss Handley. She had a brother in the Confederate army. I stole cartridges and gave them to her. She took them to Quantrill's men and kept me posted with their movements.. My father went to the Colonel of the regiment at Marshall while we were in Lexington to get me released. He told father that if he would give him $25, he would have me discharged, but nothing happened. So father went to the Provost Marshall. He told my Dad that he went to the wrong man. The Provost said that he was the only one that could have me released, so Father gave him $25 as well, but again nothing happened. Several other of the boys' fathers did the same. Nothing.

In the meantime, my brother I.C. ,who had been with Quantrill, had been wounded at Waymans in August. He was shot in the flesh part of the thigh. He sent one of the Wayman girls to Lexington to find me.

She found Miss Ann Eliza Noel, a good Southern girl whom I had visited while with the militia. She told her that our company had gone to Miami. So as soon as he was able, I. C. started for home.

Now on one Sunday in September, Miss Haynie told me that Quantrill would soon leave for the South, So A. L. Wheeler and myself went to her uncle's house where she lived and took us to a camp in the woods of Bert Markum, one of Quantrill's men. Ed Ward and Stonehouse of Company G, Gordon's Regiment talked to them and told us to wait until Tuesday evening and then come.

But A. L. Wheeler ran a race on Monday with another, and his horse fell with him and broke his collar bone. As a result, Wheeler could not go.

Mrs. Jude Smart and her daughter by a former marriage, Miss Anna, and Ella Hughes after being run from Jackson County gy General Order No. We came to Miami and were living in the old Johnson Hotel. I had frequently visited them while with the Company. As I was passing Monday morning, Miss Anna Called me in. She told me that she was leaving by boat in an hour or so for Kentucky and asked if I could go with her to the boat. So, I carried her grip to the state room. She told me that she was a sweetheart of Lt. Dickey of Quantrill, and if I met him to tell him that she had gone. Also Mrs. Judge Smart told me while her son Jim who was with Quantrill's men had gone north and wrote that it was impossible for Quantrill's to get South because the Federals were killing so fast. He decided to get away. She begged me not to go.

But I told her that I was going to try it the next day.

So, after dinner the next day (Tuesday), Captain Burnsides order all to mount horses and march to the Fair Ground to drill. I told him that I didn't have a saddle. He told me to take any saddle that I could see and come on. So, I got Jim Elson's saddle which I had always been using anyway. He had another one. We went to the Fair Ground and drilled about an hour then went back to our quarters to the river to water our horses. I left the river first, hurried to the quarters, got my clothes in a bundle, some cartridges but no gun, got on my horse, and

16

started. Captain Burnsides came as I was starting and asked, "Where to, George?"

The first thought was Mrs. Zook's (the widow who cooked for us) cow had been gone for two days and said at breakfast that she wished some of us would go hunt her up. So, I said to hunt Mrs. Zook's cow and the captain gave me permission to go.

I started on a long cow hunt but failed to find the cow but sure found trouble instead. Now several others had promised to go with me, but all backed out. Sheesh!

However, John Snelling was on picket duty and came to me as I was going to the timber southwest where the cow was supposed to be. He gave his Colts (5 shots) and a size 32 pistol belt and scabbard that he had made and wished me luck. But my Dad had given the Corporal at Marshall $25, and he will soon get me out.

I went straight down a road to the bushwhackers' camp.

We ate supper that Miss Mug Handley brought us then at dark left and went to Grand Pass. Just four of us went to Baltimore Thomas' house for breakfast. It was a large brick two story and a balcony on top ½ mile across an open field to the road. His daughter went up on top while we ate and watched for us.

Now Mr. Thomas told us that he and his family were just living on the place and for us to order what we wanted from his faithful helper who was running the place, so we always went to him and his wife who always fed and helped us the best they could.

We camped in the woods nearby until night, came back, fed the horses, got supper, and returned to our camp in the woods where I first met the bunch. We stayed all day again. Miss Haynie brought some food to us.

Now I had not enough clothes or blankets so we decided for Ward Stonehouse and I to go to my home and get supplies. We started soon after dark with me leading the way since I knew the roads in all directions, even paths.

We came to the crossing of the Miami and Marshall roads, two miles south of Miami. The Still house road we were on was only 20 feet between fences; there was no moon but clear, so one could see a short distance. I rode out in the cross roads while the others waited back 10 or 15 yards. Everything as far as I could see looked quiet. I said, "Come on boys! It's alright." When they got near me, I started in a slow trot while crossing the road.

I turned around, put my left hand on the back of the saddle, and before I could speak to the boys, shots rang out from 6 of the guys of the Militia. The first shot was so close to my head that the powder burnt the right side of my face and neck. Plus, my horse sure did jump the highest I ever had witnessed to jump. I landed behind the saddle but had caught the horn of the saddle with my right hand and pulled back into the saddle while the horse was running his best like he was in a race or something like that.

Neither of us were hurt even though they emptied all of their guns. Stone house and I were getting by Ward and turned back to go through the field to find him after daylight if possible. We stopped in the first brush which was West and slept some and was awakened just at daylight by tramping through the brush. We left our horses and crept through the brush towards the noise which we heard and soon found it was Ed Ward. We traveled back to our old camp in the hills, and Miss Haymie brought us our breakfast. She went to Miami that day and one of the man, who had been in the State Guards in 1861 and was a Southerner and forced in the Company as I had been, went to my cousin Mrs. Miller and told her that he was with them and that Jim Elson and Joe Pitman had double barreled guns and navies. The rest were muskets. He said that they all knew me, and three shot at me to kill; the other three shot into the air. I lost the pistol in the run; Scabard broke loose, but they did not find or look for him as it was found the next day by a boy and later, he sold I to William Williams who lived near. She told Miss Haynie and when she brought our supper, she told us that some of them bragged.

They sure got me but Steve Harris, the one before mentioned, told my cousin that I was not killed nor did he believe they hit me.

The next night we started again but went through fields into the brush in my father's pasture ½ mile from home in a plum thicket. About sun up I started to my sister's house, Mrs. Stipes. I met her and her husband when I crossed the pasture fence in their watermelon patch. I told them to go home and my sister Eliza to bring us our breakfast to the plum Thicket. I knew that she knew how to find us there. I took a watermelon back to our camp. It was only about two hours before my sister Eliza was there. While we were eating, she told us that our brother, I. C. was two miles behind us hunting for me and that she would hurry back to the house to get his horse and go tell him.

By noon he was with us bringing me a good, big heavy double-barreled gun. He ate dinner with us and then back to his camp to meet us at dart at Ulrey. My sister brought our supper and my clothes, etc. and told Jim Elson and near a dozen had been there and took a fine stallion from my father and said they had killed me. It excited Father but my sister Eliza said, "No, Father, they did not kill Dick." She then proceeded to tell him all about it.

We met at the appointed place and time. I piloted the squad through fields back to the Pinnacles as was the hills called Southwest of Miami. Again, Miss Haynie fed the bunch that evening. She told us that Frank Handley was coming out to see her and had two navies and that he was one of the militia. Some of us wanted to intercept him and shoot him, Bert Markum was his brother-in-law and Harve Handley was his brother. We knew that he was one of Quantrill's men. So Markum persuaded us not to bother him. Soon after, he and Miss Haynie got married, and I didn't see her again until after the war.

That night we left for Lafayette County, stayed all day near Grand Pass, and ate at B Thomas. Next, we went to near Higginsville and got one breakfast at Ja. A Lewis's house. There I met Dave Pool for the first time and also got with Lieutenant Dickey and got acquainted with Miss Juda Lewis and her sister. The next night we went to Davis Creek in Johnson County. There were now 14 of us under Dickey. The next night we started to go into Jackson County, stopped at the Wayman home for supper, and I met the girls after supper. We started on our trip near the bridge and mill on Sny-a-bar Creek. We went through the barn lot up in front of the house, and Dickey called. A young lady came out and told us there were 150 Federals camped at the mill ¼ mile from us.

I was riding with Dickey and hearing something on the outside of a fence about 50 yards away. I looked to see, and there they were trying to slip around us. I whispered to Dickey. He shouted in a loud voice, "Hurry up supper for us! We'll go to the barn, feed the horses, and come back for supper." We rode back; I got off the horse and opened the barn door. However, we went to the other door, opened it, and a gate nearby. We got on horses and we soon got away. They followed us several miles, but we went back to Davis Creek in Johnson County. The next night, my brother I. C. and some others went by a different road to Jackson County. We camped there another day and night.

Word came to us that a company of about 30 of Quantrill's men had been surprised and lost their horses and asked us to try to get some. So, Dickey and I decided to go to Miami during the night. We worked our way to the old Livery barn where the militia kept their horses and got the lot of them. I knew where all the guards were stationed and all the other seven men knew Miami well as well. We traveled all night; it rained a light shower in the night, but it was near sunup when we rode in Mrs. Foxes's pasture gate and told her to get dinner for us. We would later send for it. We went to the barn, got corn and oats, went down across a small creak near ¼ mile from the house, and fed the horses and laid down and went to sleep.

I said, "Lieutenant, hadn't we better put out a guard?' He said, "No, we need all the sleep we can get, and the Feds won't bother us here. They are afraid of Dave Pool." However, about noon we were woken up by the Feds shooting at us. So much for the guard!!!

I jumped to my feet over John Steele and had my gun in my hand. I looked towards my horse about 25 feet away and saw a gun pointing at me from both his head and tail. I jumped behind a tree as they fired. There were four of us sleeping at that big tree and four about 25 feet from us and out of sight of the one who were shooting at us, but they had divided their company of 75, part following our trail while the other going around north and coming to our camp from the opposite direction. They had evidently sent some one and found out just where we were, but the bunch that fired on us was too fast. The four of us ran East but Ryal Crowder who woke first heard them coming. He and the Feds pilot [6] both shot at each other at the same time. Crowder got his man but was not hit himself. I was the last one to leave the tree. John Steele left his gun. George McQue was just grazed by a shot.

We soon reached a high fence and came up an open field beyond except for a small patch of Osage Orange trees 10 or 12 feet high in rows four feet apart. We stopped at the grove to talk. Ryal Crowder's face was bleeding, He asked me if he had been shot bad. I looked at him saying, "No, not shot, but a bush has scratched you." John Steele turned ad asked, "Dick, am I shot bad in the nose?" I answered, "No, John, you are not shot either." He said, "Oh, I remember. I grabbed for my gun and slipped and fell against a tree and smashed my nose." Then George McQue came up saying that he had been shot bad. He was holding his right thigh. I looked and found that his pants had been torn showing a red streak but no blood. I sure had to laugh at them. John said, "Dick, it is no laughing matter. We went to the Osage Orange patch and hid there an hour or so." No more was said after that.

The others, Dickie, Ike Ulrey, Wallace Elder, and an old man ran North and into the other squad. Dickie was shot and his leg was broken in the first shots at them. He fell but shot two of them before they killed him. The others got away, but all lost horses, clothes, etc. I asked our bunch what we should do. They all seemed to be concerned as well.

Well, I am going to Lewises one mile East, get supper, and ask Miss Judy to go to Mrs. Foxes and see if the others were killed. So, it was agreed upon. I went to the house and told them, and Miss Judy

6   the person out front

got her horse and went and soon came back. I met her on the road, and she told me what had happened. The other boys would be over about dark. The foxes and Lewise girls got the boys hats and coats who had lost them, but Steele, Elder, and Ulrey had lost guns which we could not get there. When we were eating supper, Dave Pool and several of his Company came to see us. Pool said, "What do you boys propose to do now?" I was next to the youngest, so he asked the older ones first. He then turned to me and said, "Dick, what do you intend to do?" I said, "I am going to Saline and get a horse and bedding, etc." He answered, "Good, you are right. Dan, you go there and back?" I said, yes." Then he said, "I appoint you in command to lead them there, mount and back. Get here, and I will meet you next Monday night, and we will go South."

Now I had learned when I knew the direction to travel by the stars when I could see them. So that night I started with the six others through fields. At daylight we were going out of B. Thomas's field across a road into the timber and met a black man. I think he was with Thomas. I asked him if they were up. He said, "I just left there." I sent the boys to camp in the woods nearby and went and ordered our breakfast and told of meeting the old man. Yes, he just left here, but be sure to go to the church. There a Company of Feds there, so you boys get back as soon as possible.

I soon had our breakfast in some papers, went to camp, and we ate as we went down the bluff and waded through the lake. The old man told me that when we got back there in about an hour, the Feds were there but did not find out how we got away.

We went to the back of a Mr. Little's farm. I walked up to the house on the river bank and got our supper, but old Mr. Black and George McQue said they would go to Carroll Company, get horses, and meet me near Mr. Little's place on our return, but they never showed up. Hmmmmmm....

We traveled through timber most of the afternoon. Soon after dark, and Wallace Elder, being near his home, went there promising to meet me Saturday night at the widow Haynie and to get her son, who was hiding in the bush near her home, to meet us. We went through fields and woods just a straight course, and at daylight I went into camp in Oscar Davis's pasture near the old school Spring. I went up to the house and got Oscarto to go to my Dad's house ½ mile East to tell my sister, Eliza. She soon came to the spring. I met her, and she brought us something to eat. She let the other boys know where we were and came to see. I told her to go to Thomas Winning's place, ten miles away, and get a mare of Brother Nat's and an overcoat.

She got a neighbor boy about eight years old to go with her. He rode behind her. She got the mare, saddle and bridle, and a fine gray overcoat with a big cape and folded it up around her under dress. She also had a big blanket under her saddle and one under the saddle the boy was riding which was my horse. On the way she met Captain Burnsides with his company. She and the boy rode out to give them the road. She told Captain Burnsides good evening and spoke to all she knew as they passed.

The next day she made arrangements for horses for John Steele and Ike Ulrey and told John that he could find a gun in Steve Wheeler's barn at a certain place Harry Wheeler had hold her. That night as we were leaving, Rile Crawdue left us saying that he was going north.

We loaded up all our blankets on my horse at dark plus a sack of oats, went a mile south, and 1/2 mile south to get the gun for Steele then west and north to Miami Road as I wanted to bid my old sweetheart Ella Thomas good bye and take a message to her brother with Shelby. It was 10pm when we got there. I rode up to the house and called her. She and her mother came to the door to bid me goodbye and told me what to tell Harvey. He was killed about ten days after in Shelby's fight at Marshall.

We rode through fields to Mrs. Haynies's house about 1am, but neither Wallace Elder nor Ott Haynie was there, so we went on to Mr. Littles's house near noon. He had not seen or heard of Black and McQue. We got supper at Mr. Thomas's house, and I gave the old man a half dollar to help us through fields across the Marshall and Waverly roads which I considered our most dangerous part of the trip. I travelled by the stars after old man got as far as he knew. We got within ½ mile of Lewis before daylight. We were sleepy, so we slept an hour or so, went to the house, got breakfast, but they told us Dave Pool and Company left at 10pm. The boys were so discouraged that I had to beg them to go on with me in daylight. We then traveled to Mrs. Fox's house. She told us that they left there at 12 midnight.

We started to knowing they would go to or near our former camp on Davis Creek, but it sure would be a risk in daylight. As we started our, a little girl passed us. She talked to her grandmother, Mrs. Fox, and she called me back and said, "Mr. Cruzen, my granddaughter tells me that Lt. Greenwood and Fotch McFadden were just leaving my daughter's when she started. Was only ¼ mile so I rode up to the house and asked about them." He said that I don't know anything about them, but after talking a few minutes, he said that he would go with us and see if he could find them. He only went a short distance in the woods and told us to stop. He went a short distance. I could hear them talking. Greenwood called me to come, and the other boys came in a few minutes. We stayed there until about noon and then rode to Pools on Davis Creek but East of where I had been before. We got there about 3pm.

Pool put me on picket but in about two hours relieved me, and we started for Quantrill's rendezvous on Blackwater in the northwest corner of Johnson County. We got there about sun up just as they were forming to start. As we came my brother I. C. came to meet us, and we went with him to Bill Greens Company. We marched all day South through Pleasant Hill. We stopped before sun down, fed the horses, and ate what we had brought. We then slept a few hours and then we were up and gone again. There were over 400 of us.

Now I can't remember the days we were on the ride, but our men ran out of grub. We were north of Carthage about 10 or 15 miles going west down a creek and the word was passed back to go to the mill just north of the road and get flour if there was any there. Then we were going to stop soon for breakfast. I went to the Mill, but all the flour was in the bin and covered with dust. I brushed the dust back and scooped up a gallon or so in my sack. We soon stopped. My brother, I. C., worked up the dough; I picked out the worms, some were an inch long, but we were hungry. We cooked it on a stick, and it tasted good even if we didn't have any salt or grease in it.

We soon left camp. I guess it was the 9th of October of 1863. We traveled west down the creek, and sometime later the word was passed back to keep closed up. We were in a brisk run with Todds Company in front. Soon we heard a few shots, and we passed a dead man and a wagon loaded with a house torn to pieces. We soon saw another and another and the last at the creek, and a few Feds that were with the wagons.

We did not slack up but rushed up the steep hill and formed a line then charged the fort at Baxter Springs. We did not try to take the fort but passed around it on both sides. Captain Green and six or eight men saw a few Feds ide in a small hazel brush patch southwest of the fort. We rode around and found seven. Dave Ferril and I were guarding them with Quantrill called to fall in northwest of us.

Green said, "Shoot those men and come on!" But I rode away and left them for I could not shoot a prisoner. As I got in line Quantrill ordered us to charge. It was General Blunt and his body guard who all formed alike before we had known they were near. He had 97 men and only 17 got away. Blunt was one of them. With all this fighting, we had one man killed, Bill Bledsaw. John Kroger wounded bad, and Captain Asa Thompson was shot in his hand.

While we were charging, I saw Bill Bledsaw get shot. He was to my left about 20 or 30 feet. I turned my head and saw the man that shot him in the Band wagon and was trying to get to him, so I could shoot him, but he was shot by someone else. In a few minutes the 12 band men were all dead. While this so-called race was happening, one wheel of the wagon had broken off and that stopped their run. I picked up and E flat Bugle. I first thought that I'd keep it, but thought I could not keep my gun with it, so I threw it away. As of this writing, I am sorry that I had done that.

My brother, I. C., who was west of me and several men, followed on in the chase. He came back with his sawed-off musket and two britch loading Kerril rifles, three navies, and a lot of ammunition for them. He gave me one rifle and one navie. I gave my shot gun to Ike Ulray.

We got some bacon and hard tack out of Blunts' wagons, so we had supper that night. We got no more to eat until we got to some Indian Reservation South of the Canadian River. We had little sleep as well. We crossed the Arkansas River above the mouth of the Canadian River and camped south of South Canadian about sundown and found a field of corn. We fed our horses. I partly roasted an ear of corn and ate it. We were about worn out, and the first I knew in the morning, my brother I.C. was pulling at me and said, "Get up; we are surrounded." I got up, put a saddle on my horse, but forgot to untie her. When I found all were leaving me, I came to my senses, untied my horse and was soon in line. But it was Texas and the Indian Confederates not Feds. We found it by leaving John Kroger in the ambulance. When we fell back to form, they ran up to him, and he, with his navie, demanded to know who they were. When they said Southern soldiers, he hollered and said to tell Quantrill quick before they get to shooting.

We soon marched on to their camp and rested one day and two nights. Then we marched on to Bonham, Texas where we went into Camp Northeast about five miles, and Captain Green communicated to Shelby that about 50 under him was waiting orders from him. However, Shelby had not returned from his raid to Missouri, and we did not get orders for some time. In about ten days our drinking water became so foul from leaves in the bayou that we were moved five miles Southwest of Bonham to a big lake. There was an approach out in the lake made of poles laid close together. It was so muddy near the water that there was danger of poisoning the stock. I counted 16 carcasses of cattle in mud one day, yet that seemed to be all the water we could get. In about two weeks, Shelby ordered us to Clarksville and rest up until further orders. We camped just Northeast of Clarksville on the creek. We had plenty of good water there and good beef and flour and sure enjoyed the time there. We got orders to join Shelby five miles Northwest of Washington, Arkansas and arrived there around Christmas Eve. Seven of us joined E Company, Gordon's Regiment. The rest scattered throughout the other companies. Most however stayed with Captain Green in Shanks Regiment.

There we found our grub, corn meal, and poor beef. It was all what we got for months. The seven of us went into the Miami mess making it 16 strong and sure fine bunch of boys, but the rest of the company were just as good. About the last day of December, Coloney Shelby started towards Camden, Arkansas. That night it rained then turned to snow, and we hd about three inches of snow over us in the morning. It was cold with some sleet after we got up and that soon froze a hard crust, so we stayed that day with dried out blankets, etc.

One of our men who went for corn saw a fine turkey on the way as he was coming back. He had on an overcoat with a big cape. As it was getting dark, he rode up, put his arm over the turkey, and brought it to camp. I was chosen to dress it. We sure had a feast of stewed turkey. YUM! The next day we marched toward Camden. That night John Steele and I went out for corn. He had a blanket and a gunny sack to fill.

The Brigade ferage master had men counting it out in piles in the barn lot, and the Regiment foragers counted out those piles to ears. The lot was full of men waiting their turn. In piling the corn around the ground was strewn with grain. I noticed a fine goose picking it up between my feet and John Steeles its head toward John. I said in a low voice for him to hold down his sack, and as he did, I kicked the goose until it walked into his sack. He asked, "What do I do now?" I simply told John to go to camp, and I'll bring your corn. So, he went. No one else say what we had done. When I got to camp, they were cooking it. Sure, was fine!

In due time, we got to Camden and reported to General Holmes and to Marmaduke.

The next day all the Cavalry started north on Pine Bluff Road, but we stopped at the Saline River and sent out scouts collecting flour, bacon, and beef cattle. Some went in a few miles of Pine Bluff but had no engagements. In a few days, a detail of ten men under LT. John Flenner Company was ordered to report to General Holmes, Dave Ferril, and I from Company E. The Department Commissary had about 20 wagons loaded with bacon, flour, sweet potatoes, etc. We guarded them to Camden making it a four-day trip. Within this Commissary was a fine man and his cook who fixed us dinner. We lived fine on that trip.. When we got to Camden, the Post Commander sent us to a vacant house to stay in until the Command got back. We got rations from the post.

My but it was poor beef and poor course corn meal. We had no cooking vessels of any kind, so I went to a lady back of us and borrowed some. She sent us several times nice roasted port and pies. We got to be good friends. Her husband had a lot of hounds, and a few miles above Camden was a big cane break along the river. There were wild hogs in it, but one could find them without the hounds. He told me that sny time I would come, he would go with me and get a hog. But the Brigade came back, and we went into winter quarters Southeast of Camden about two miles. We made log shelters covered with blankets so nicely fixed, but oh the grub we got. Super yummy!!

One day Thom Ingram and I got passes to go hunting. The passes did not allow us to go to Camden, but in my four days there, I learned where all the guards were. So, we went a block around and stopped on Main Street in ½ block of General Holmes Office, bought some homemade beer and ginger cakes, then went to get my friend along with his hounds. His wife told us that he was already hunting and thought we could find him by the hounds' running. But we failed to find him and started back empty. We went south a mile to miss Camden. Going through a lane, the house on the south and barn on north, five hogs started running before us. When they would stop, we would say, "Boo! Boo!" So, we drove them through the lane and into the woods. I rode ahead of one and it stopped, looked at me, and I shot it with my navie. In a few minutes we had it cut up so we could put it in our sack and started for camp. When we were nearly there and in a narrow road in the timber, we met General Holmes and his escort. I said give the road and salute the General and we did. H returned our salute and passed on. It was a close call, but we got by and ate pork that night.

About the second week in February 1864, our Regiment was sent to picket the Saline River with Colonel Gordon's quarters in Princeton. Company E was sent to a ferry on Pine Bluff Road. We had a four-room log house and barn for horses. We got good grub while there, and the neighbors were friendly to us. One day some of the boys found a vacant house a mile south and a lot of chickens around. That night at dark, we raided it and brought in two dozen fine hens. It was my turn to cook and had borrowed cooking vessels when we first went there. Before I had them cooked, two neighbor men came in to talk. I had to set the pots off the fire but kept them covered up until they left. My, but we did eat them. Afterwards we found that they belonged to one of our best neighbors, daughter, and her husband. He was in the army east of the Mississippi River, but we never let them know that we got their chickens.

Early in April, Lt. Bob Thompson and ten men of our Company went across the river. My brother I. C. and I went with the bunch and four or five Arkansas men went with us. We moved on to what they called an island, but we were not surrounded by water but nearly as a bayou. On the south side, the Arkansas men went to a friend planter's house south of the bridge near the mouth of the bayou. In the morning, he told us to come for supper and he would have a treat. He sent his 15-year-old son with some cotton to Pine Bluff about four miles below the river. He sold the cotton, got a gallon of whiskey, a dozen hats, a dozen fine calf boots, and some shirts. We had a fine supper, hot milk punch, and I got a hat and a pair of boots which I needed. Then the Arkansas men crossed the river. I seemed to be the only one that knew how to manage a skiff, so I had to go with them to bring the boat back.

It clouded up while we were crossing, so I could not see anything to tell where I was landing as I got back.

I pulled the boat to the bank of the river; it seemed to run up on the bank. I had my gun strapped over my shoulder including my navie and nearly 100 rounds of cartridges on my belt. I put oars on the edge of the boat and stepped out with my right foot, but it was only drift trash below some logs and as the trash gave way, my leg slipped into water clean up to my thigh. To keep from falling in the river, I threw myself backwards into the bottom of the boat, but the fall sent the boat out into the current. Unfortunately, the river was very high. I got one oar but had lost the other one. Plus, it was so dark that I could not see it. With the one oar, I pulled back to the bank and got out and tied it to a bush. I was sure a close call. I went to the old ferryman's house who had drifted down ¼ mile and told him about what happened. He said, "I have no other oar." I asked, "Haven't you a thick stout board and a drawing knife?" He answered, "I have the knife but only 1 ½ inch cotton board." He got it, and we soon had another oar. However, it was rather weak. I said, "I'll keep this on the upper side of the boat, and it will be O.K." He agreed, "You are right?" Some of us got in, and I took over then went back to get the rest. It had cleared off, and the moon was just about setting. We had left our horses hidden back in the woods.

We walked about three miles down the river to a big plantation that had been vacated when the Feds came, but a carpetbagger had brought some horses as well as some men that he hired to raise cotton. Lt. Thompson and I went into one of the cabins. An old man and his wife were in there. I saw a sewed-up shirt of homespun cotton on a table, rolled it up, and put it in my pocket. I took the old man outside to guard as directed. I stepped back to speak to the Lieutenant; the old man jumped the rail fence and ran stooping so low that the fence would protect him. He would not stop, and the Lieutenant told me to shoot him. He dropped down as I shot but did not get up. I never knew if I had killed him or not; I hoped not.

We got about a dozen good horses and some of the boys too two young boys. We had heard there was Company of Feds a mile from the Plantation camped in a school house, so we lost no time in getting back to our crossing on the river. At daylight I started with my first load, one man in the stern, and seven horses which he was leading.

Near the center of the river, the horses circled as on both sides of the boat and tried to climb in. I hit them over the head with an oar and turned them away from the boat and soon had them over. I returned and got two more men and the rest of the horses. I. C. and Thomas Ingram started back, and a steamboat came down just as we landed but there were Feds on. So, we let it alone. They let us go, but we saw a lot of dust stirred up on the North side of the river. We thought it was the Feds from the school house, so we hollered for the two boys to hide, but it was about six or eight men and 100 mules. As soon as they passed, I went back for the boys and got Thomas Ingram, but I. C. had hidden so well that we did not find him, so we came back without him. We then went to our horses but first I went to the old ferryman and got him to promise to go get I. C. when he came out on to the beach. Lt. Thompson wanted to go and leave my brother, I said that I will go back to the ferry for him at dark. We had crossed the bayou and gone two miles to rest and slept some.

Thomas Ingram went back with me and the ferryman had gotten I. C.; He was sleeping in his barn. We soon were back in camp and started to the Saline River. We got there the next day, but our Company had gone. We stayed that night near our old camp, got breakfast from one of our friends, and started to Camden. We met a farmer coming. He said, "General Steele is in Camden, and you are ½ mile of his pickets." We turned back and went East down the river about ten miles and crossed on a pontoon bridge that the Confederates made and ran into Shelby's brigade. We had missed the fighting in Steele's rear and at Prairie Ran and Poison Spring. The second day after we got to our command, we were ordered to report to General Fagan, but the men were mad because they all loved Marmaduke. Shelby said, "It is alright.

When we get through with Steele, we will get to northern Arkansas, and I'll be in command of all there."

Late in the afternoon, we crossed the river with four brigades and travelled most of the night. It was dark and rainy but cleared up around sun up. We started North, and it wasn't long until we heard shooting in the front. Our Regiment was in front of the Brigade and Shelby was just before us. General Fagan stopped at a cross road, and he told Shelby to that road. He said that it was 15 miles around and was wondering if he could make it within an hour. He replied that he would do it. This was called the Marks Mills Battle.

When we got in front of the Feds, one shot was fired to let Fagan know that we had gotten there. Fagan charged their rear, but we were so far from them. Fagan came near but was being defeated before we could get back to them. Ten men were sent out under Lt. Flener. I. C. was with them; they rode so fast that another bunch was sent under Haynie. Dave Ferril and I were also with that bunch. The first bunch began firing on the wagons, etc. capturing all of them. The Feds began to break, and our first advance captured two pieces of artillery, the other four. So many horses and men were killed; they did not move.

I rode out of the woods into a road beside an open field and could see Feds running all over the field. I halted and the nearest one surrendered and gave me his gun and ammunition. About that time Colonel Gordon passing the road. I told him, "Colonel I have a prisoner." He said, "Darn! Shoot him and come on!" They have just shot Joe Alumban after he had surrendered which was the fact. My brother I. C. was 20 feet ahead of me and saw and heard it all. He ran behind a big tree, and approximately 40 or 50 Feds shot at him but hit the tree. I turned to my prisoner and said, "No, I never shoot a prisoner."

Dave Ferril, just 50 or 60 feet from us, also had prisoner. I marched him to Dave and a Lt. raised up out the weeds and said, "I have 25 men that we will surrender to you if you will guard us." I said, "Sure, I will." I formed them in line and marched back to the battlefield with Dave behind and I in front. Others turned prisoners of me, and when we got to General Shelby, I had about 75. I simply told him that I had some prisoners. He told me to turn them over to Captain Rathburn while pointing to him nearby. I then asked the General if we should go to our Regiment. He told me that I probably not be able to find them. They were gathering up more prisoners. He additionally told me that I could go over to where the battle field was and then go north on the road to the creek. He and his men were going to camp there that night and perhaps I could find my Regiment there. When we arrived, we found wagons and a few there.

The next day we moved west near Arkadelphia to get corn and provisions and stayed there two nights. We then started back travelling most of the night in a hard rain. We got to Jenkins Ferry just as the fight was over and went over the field and saw the dead and wounded lying in the mud everywhere both Blue and Gray. However, Steele had gotten away.

We went west next day near Arkadelphia, camped on a high ridge, and while there Dave Pool came with his Company from Louisiana and was ordered to join our Regiment. I went to visit them that first night as I knew most all of them. Pool said, "Dick, do you want to go to Missouri with me? I am going in a few days." I said, No, Captain. I had rather stay where I am, but will you take a letter to my sister, Margaret?" He answered, "Sure I'll be down in Saline County sometime soon after. After I get there just write it and give it to Ambros Maxwell. He'll take care of it." I told I. C., so we both wrote and Poole and Ambros took them to her in June, the first word they had from us since I left in October.

Early in May, Shelby broke camp and started for North Arkansas. The rivers and creeks were full of water, and the roads were bad. We travelled alongside the Arkansas River but very little fighting took place. I was in the skirmish line while dismounted and going through thick brush. It was dark and raining with only a mist. The rest were sent west and did most of all the fighting. We could hear the guns for some time but saw no one to shoot at. Finally, were halted, and it soon began to get light. I had just entered the clearing west of the town and about 50 feet in front was the corner of the stockade fort.

We rode into camp, fed the horses, got breakfast, and Sgt. Thomas Ingram and seven of our Company were ordered to report to Shelby. He gave us orders to go up the river for ten miles and see if we could locate a boat. We found one flat boat on the north side of the river 10 miles back and reported to Shelby. He sent a company after it that night.

Soon after we got back in camp and when cooking supper, Captain Elliott came to me and said, "George, Colonel Gordon wants to see you." When I got to him, he handed me a bugle and said, "Can you blow that?" I looked it over the mouth piece was gone. I told him that I thought it was very doubtful. He said, "Try it." So, I blew assembly but rather poorly. He said, "That will do. Go get your horse and outfit and come here." I asked, "Colonel, must I bring my gun?" He said, "No, give it to one of the boys." I was many times sorry I gave it away.

We crossed the river the next day and marched to Batesville. One night, I molded a lead mouth piece, dug a hole in the ground, sharpened a stick, and stuck it in the ground then melted a few minnies balls and pour them in holes. I trimmed it with my knife to fit in the bugle then trimmed the inside to give a proper sound.

My horse died one night while up in the mountains on their trip, and I was forced to ride a mule that the company gave me to ride all summer. Our Regiment went into camp on White River below Batesville. Jackman's brigade was formed, and Shanks was put in command of the old brigade.

In about 10 days we started for Clarendon on White River because we were going into camp one night. Colonel Shanks stopped our regiment and said, "Gordon, have your regiment camp the right of the road along the creek, and while going into camp come here in the shade and rest." Jim Webb, Gordon's orderly lined up the regiment for camp, and Colonels Gordon and Blackwell, Captain Red, and I got off our horses by Colonel Shanks.

He said, "do you know where we are going?"

Gordon said, "No."

Shanks said, "Well, we are going to Clarendon to capture a gunboat."

Gordon said, "You ought not to tell what we are going to try to do." Shanks remarked, "This bunch knows enough not to tell. Plus, if I am going to be wounded, it won't be bad, but we will go to Missouri in the fall. It is possible that I will be either killed or wounded, so I will never get back into service."

We had bayous and muddy swamps to go through which made progress somewhat slow.

We went into camp 1 ½ miles from Clarendon early afternoon, killed some beaver, got supper, and went to sleep. About midnight, we heard the other regiments moving out, and some of them asked us what regiment we were. We told them Gordon's. They said, "You're Shelby's pets; he doesn't take them to fight gunboats. Just at daylight we heard our four guns boom, a few small guns, and it was all over. The gunboat was disabled by of the guns, so they could do a thing with it. A steam pope was shot also. Then they surrendered."

Our regiment moved about ½ mile nearer and rested then got breakfast. I started to make a pair of pants of which I had gotten cut out, but soon we heard the boom of more and bigger guns and some shells came near us. Three gunboats and some transports had come from Duvalls Bluff, 15 miles up the river, and began shelling our battery. Shank was slightly wounded in the thigh by a piece of shell. We burned the boat that we had captured before the gunboats got there. We retreated, but Gordon's regiment covered the retreat. We had a stiff fight to hold the infantry back from the transports while Shelby got away. The regiment lost several good men and more were wounded. Their Calvary followed us until night with skirmishes every few miles.

We had about five miles of swamp to go through before we crossed the Cache River. The other regiments went on and left the cannons mired in mud. Gordon ordered 50 men to help them out, but soon Gordon sent 20 men for each gun. We were stopped behind the last gun. I said to Him Webb, "I am so sleepy that I am going to sleep on my mule." He said, "alright. I can't sleep riding, so I'll watch you." Finally, I woke up and realized that his horse and my mule were eating grass beside the road. We had passed all the guns and probably rode two miles while we slept. Yepper, both of us had been asleep on our mounts. We went onto the river and the last of the regiments were ahead getting onto the ferryboat. When we got nearly across, we saw General Shelby watching the men as they left the boat. Webb and I shifted to the other side of boat, so we had a man between us and the General. We went about ½ mile into a cornfield, laid down, and slept until daylight, and then the regiment came up. Gordon had missed us but laughed when I told him about what happened. We again went into camp on White River at the ford below Batesville.

In a few days about the first week of June, Jim Webb asked Colonel Gordon for a pass to visit relatives a few miles across the river. Gordon asked, "who will fill your job while you are gone?" Jim said, "Dick will." Gordon said, "alright, he can fill both jobs." I told Gordon that I would be happy to help Jim out.

Well, Jim never made it back. It was reported that he was either killed or captured. About the last of June, our regiment was ordered to report to Colonel Dobins, 25 miles west of Helena. Before we left, I asked Colonel Gordon if he had not best get another orderly. He wanted to know if I was getting tired of the job. I told him that I was a Confederate soldier and will always be ready to do the limit where best I can serve. He said, "that settles it. There is no man in the regiment who can fill the place as well as you."

After a few days march late in the evening, the Colonel dropped back leaving me in front. We came out in an old abandoned field, we came upon some delicious blackberries. They were everywhere!! I left the road and grabbed a handful; the men all followed suit.

The Colonel then came up to me and yelled, "What in the heck are you doing, Dick? I want you to understand that when I leave, you are in command, and I want the regiment to know that they are to obey you as they do me. If you ever do this sort of thing again, it will sure go hard with you."

I rode back by his side, and the regiment followed. We went into camp near there, and he said, "don't be hurt by what I said to you. I don't blame you, but I had to whip the men over your shoulders, I and I wanted to let them know that they must obey you as you will always know what I want done."

I went back with a big pan and got a lot of berries along with Major George Crowdon's helper, Lee, who sure made us a good pie for supper.

The evening of the first day of July as we were going into camp with Colonel Dobins as we turned off the road ¼ mile to camp, I noticed an old man and a black boy sitting on top of a rail fence with a big watermelon each beside them and a big field of corn behind them. We went into camp. I took a sack, went by Company E, told John Steele to get a sack and go with me. He got one, and as we went back, he was wanting to know what was going on. I asked him if he saw that old man with the young black boy on the fence with watermelons. John concurred. Now how were we going to get some? That was the next question. When we got to the fence, the man and boy were both gone. So, we just started following their tracks. We followed them about 150 yards when we found an acre of watermelons. We got four fine ones when we met up with two other men going on the same errand. I also noticed that the corn looked nice. Good for roasting. So, we got some of those too and put them on top of the watermelons. What a load we had! By the time we got to camp, we were exhausted. But I figured it was all worth it.

Also, when we got back to camp, there were two old citizens talking with Colonel Gordon. I laid my sack down a few feet from them, and pretty soon Colonel Blackwell sat down on it. I just gently pushed his thigh lightly and quietly said, "Colonel, you may bruise those roasting ears." I had to hold my tongue to keep from laughing. He slid off the sack, but the two men left. He then grabbed the sack and wanted to know what was in it. To make a long story short here, we had quite a feast!

The second evening after supper, we all started towards Helena. Dobins had ten men in advance and our regiment was next. He rode with Colonel Gordon, and I was next behind them. He halted us about 1 am and rode up to a house. He knew the people well. The told him about 1000 Feds with two cannons had passed there about 9pm going to get him and his men, but they took the south road. We had come from the north road. We turned around, and 900 men followed them. They went into camp at the creek in a fort called Bacon two miles from the camp that we had left the night before. They sent 100 cavalry to see just where Dobins was and did not know our regiment was already there.

Dobins sent our regiment to the west and McGee's battalion to the east. He attacked while we were dismounting. Colonel Gordon and I, in front, turned around the corner of a fence into the road two hundred yards from the fort going in a run. They turned towards us with guns firing at us only missing Gordon a few feet. He said, "Dick, form the regiment in a straight line." In five minutes, we were charging through the timber with them firing at us. We got to a branch 150 yards from them and then circled around to the creek bank west of there along with trees, logs, and banks to help us hold the line. I went all around our line helping to carry Lt. Lankford out of danger when he was shot in the stomach. I then went back to Colonel Gordon in the hollow where the road crossed and stayed until the fight was over while their two guns continued to fire at our sharp shooters who was behind trees in front of us.

Their scouts heard the firing just as they got to our camp and turned back without taking the few men who were prisoners or destroying anything. Our boys there said that they were scared to death and sur was glad when we got back that night. We had used most of our ammunition. When their scout got to the bridge, they found Dobins between it and fort. They went east and crossed and went around to the road. They had come from Helena and attacked McGhee at his rear; he gave way to the east in the woods, and they rode into the fort.

Immediately they all started on the run back to Helena and got out where McGhee vacated his line. We were ordered to our horses and went as fast as we could through woods and a road to head them off. We went 14 miles, but Dobins did not get in striking distance of their rear so they got back. We left a lot of their dead and wounded along with their wagons but kept their guns. Only one of our regiments was wounded; none killed but Dobins had quite a lot.

The second day in the evening, we started again. Colonel Gordon was sick, so Colonel Blackwell commanded our regiment.

About sunup we ran the pickets at east of Helena then went east down the river and raided Colonel Dobins and a lot of other plantations on the island as it was called being a big bayou on the west. Our regiment was in front. When we got near the east end, Colonel Blackwell told me there was a foot bridge across the bayou, and we must get it and that there was a stockade fort with 16 black soldiers guarding it. He said, "Call for two volunteers to charge it." But none volunteered, so I encouraged the men to have one go with me to charge that fort. Will Perce, a new recruit, rode to me. He had a long gun; I had my navie. As we turned the corner, I pointed to the fort and said, "Will, we probably both will be shop from our horses before we get there, but the regiment will get there before they load their guns." I rode in the gate, but no one was there then we went to the bridge. I led my mule across the boards which were nailed to logs that were floating and tied to a big grapevine across. They sank under the water about an inch. I told him to follow 10 or 12 feet back. All crossed that was safe, and as the last were going up the bluff, gunboat commenced shelling the bridge. We got back to camp that night with some good horses. In a few days our regiment went back to our camp on White River near Batesville.

A few days after being in camp, General Shelby rode up to Gordon's headquarters with a paper in his hand and said," Gordon, here is a challenge I got today from the colonel of the 10th Illinois Calvary. Read it." It asked Shelby to send 1000 men to fight his 1000. Shelby asked, "how many men do you have? Gordon replied, "500." Shelby said, "If I give you Williams' battalion plus one or two other companies to give you 900, will you go meet him?" Gordon answered excitedly, "Yes, sir. I sure will." We started at night and rode the whole time. Williams charged with his 400 across the big bridge while we went around and crossed at a fort, hitched our horses, and crept through the brush at day light, but Williams was too fast for us. He charged into their camp, killed a few, and the rest got to their horses and ran away. We got some horses, a few prisoners, and some wagons then headed back to our camp.

About July20th, Shelby's division all marched to the Railroad between Duvals Bluff and Little Rock expecting to meet General Price with Marmaduke's and Fagan's Divisions. We were scattered along the road several miles and captured several forts with little fighting and burned lots of hay. Jackman, east of our line, ordered Colonel Mitchel to surrender. He was in a hay bale fort with over 400 men. He wrote a note back to Jackman that he did not what surrender meant. Jackman sent the letter to Shelby saying they were two or three miles from us. Being upset with this news, Shelby ordered us to go there with our battery. We went on the run. The battery was put in position in front of our regiment. It soon set fire to the hay, and Mitchel's men took to the railroad ditches. Our regiment was dismounted and started charging. A lot of the men got out of the ditches and waved white handkerchiefs which meant surrender. Mitchel tried to take the handkerchiefs, but more men joined. We stopped 100 yards from them and sent a squad to receive their surrender and marched them off. In going back to my mule, I went to a tent made of Government blankets buttoned together. I cut two of them out, got two blankets, and ran to my mule. When I was tying them behind my saddle, we were ordered to fall in behind Hunter's regiment which was being rushed by Missouri Feds. We were ordered to retreat, but they were crowding us. Ike Shelby got our flag, stood up in his saddle, and shouted, "Come on boys!" Lieutenant Perry Catron wheeled his horse around and hollered at us about the Feds coming at us. I blew the charge and all joined, even Colonel Gordon.

We drove them across the railroad, and they did not follow us. It was open level prairie. We fell back in a walk in a line. Colonel Gordon rode up to me and said, "who gave you orders to sound the charge?" I said that I heard Ike Shelby and Perry Catron say charge. He laughed and then said that it turned out to be the proper thing to do.

General Price did not meet us but sent a carrier that he was coming west of Little Rock. We retreated with our 500 or 600 prisoners back into the timber, camped for the night, and moved out at sunup. Our regiment was to guard the rear as usual in time of danger. At a big bayou ten or twelve miles from camp, the Feds ran our rear-guard inward. We crossed the big bridge and waited for them. Soon they came in a charge, but one round sent them back a little. Some of them crossed but did not attack us. We retreated slowly, but they still did not follow.

We went back to camp and in a few days got orders to march slowly north up the Black River. About the second night, we camped by a corn field in the river bottom. It commenced to rain slowly. I fixed some flat rails with one end up off the round, got some corn stalks to put on top, and stretched up my rubber blanket and cape then put my overcoat above me. Then I noticed Colonel Blackwell sitting on his saddle propped against a tree. I said, "Here Colonel, come in my so-called tent." He got up, looked, and said, "It looks good, but I don't want to rob you of your nice nest." I answered, "Oh, come on. I got room for you." So, after that, we bunked together. I told him that I would get him some blankets while in Missouri. We moved slowly several days until Price caught up with us near Fredricks Town Company. I and H. were ordered to report to Shelby early one morning. I got permission to go with them. Our orders were to avoid a fight if we could find out all we could.

Within a few miles east of Farmington, an old man met us and asked, "Why don't you go whip them Feds in Farmington?" He told us that there were about 75. We also had about the same number of men. Captain Chrispin, in command, said that it was against orders or he would do just that. Captain Moreman told Chrispin to take command.

Chrispin decided to leave it to a vote of the men. All agreed to give them a round. So, Chrispin went as a private. One mile from the courthouse was a toll gate at the end of the Pike Road. The tollman closed the gate and requested toll from us. Captain Moreman turned to Lieutenant John Flenner whom I was riding next to. Moreman said to take three men and lead the advance. We drew our navies, and Flenner said to open the gate. He did, and we started in a run. The two companies followed close. The Feds were in the courthouse, a good brick one. Two men on horses were out front. Flenner and I chased them over a mile but they had the fastest horses, so we turned back. Meanwhile, our boys had taken to other buildings and were sharp shooting. Three others met us a block from the courthouse, and Captain Chrispin sent Mark Morgan to order us back around a block from the courthouse. As he got to where we were close together talking, a man shot at us from a hold in the roof of the courthouse. I looked up and saw where he was and, in a few seconds, saw his gun coming out of the hole. I got the first shot, and he jumped back. I said, "Boys, go and keep him from shooting until I empty my gun." At that point I hid. Then I started to shoot but Morgan had waited for me and followed me. In passing a block south and in full view for him, he shot twice at me but missed, but he grazed Morgan's chest. When I got back to the companies, one of Company H's men told me that there was young lady a block south that wanted to see me. I went and if I have not got her and another lady I met at Independence the same way. I may have gotten her mixed up with Miss Ann Eliza Noel of Lexington. As we drew away, a Company of Shank's regiment and Sam Hildebrand's bushwhackers came in on the west and demanded a surrender. They surrendered and were taken to Shelby. We got back to camp that night.

The next night, Shelby sent Colonel Gordon an order for ten picked men who were best armed and mounted. Colonel handed me the order to read. I asked the Colonel, "Must I pick those men or let the Captains pick?" He replied, "Dick, you know the men; you may pick them." To begin with I chose my brother, Ikie, then Thom Ingram from

Company E and Al Jeffries from Company A. I couldn't remember the others, but all had Sharps rifles or guns that used Sharps cartridges. All had two navies and 30 others were similarly armed under A. McCoy who led our advance from there on.

Within a few days, we struck the Iron Mountain Railroad not far from Caledonia. Only the advance got into a skirmish with soldiers on a train going east. It soon got out of reach. We destroyed the road for miles. Our regiment went to Caledonia and camped for the night. Our doctors got there with some medicine and some whiskey. We spent several days moving near the road and a short distance north. One day while on a march, I noticed my brother, Ikie, lying down beside the road holding his horse. I went to him and found him to be very sick. I stopped our ambulance. [7] It was full of sick men. I asked Dr. Wood who was in charge if I could get my brother in the ambulance. He told me that it was full and to get him to a house and leave him. I vehemently said, "NO!" Besides If I left him, I insisted that I would stay with him. I then asked the sick men if anyone was able to ride. One of them said yes if he had a horse. I simply told him to get on my brother's horse, and we then put Ikie in the ambulance. That night we camped in Petosi, but the regiment started to Pilot Knob but left our ambulance and the sick men under the care of Dr. Brown. He soon was dead drunk. Ikie was so sick that I went to Dr. Fulkerson who was in charge of Shank's sick and got him to see Ikie. He gave me some medicine for him, and in the morning, I went again to see Dr. Fulkerson. He gave me more medicine and asked me if I knew what Dr. Wood had given him, but all I knew was whiskey. I had a canteen full of it of which Dr. Wood told me to get and give it to Ikie every few hours. So, Sr. Fulkerson said to give him plenty of it; it is about all he needs for a few days.

That evening we got orders to march and to get with our regiment. We traveled most of the night. It was dark and raining. Once the ambulance with four sick and the drunk Dr. Brown turned over in the ditch. We pulled them out and got the ambulance up on the road. Thank goodness

---

7   ambulance – covered wagon used as a traveling hospital

no one was hurt, so we proceeded onward. We got with our regiment the next norming. We did not go far that day, however; my brother was much better. We moved north the next day, and before we started to move, we got orders for Lt. John Flenner and ten men to scout Northeast of Union. I asked Col. Gordon if I could go, and he allowed it.

I rode Ikie's horse on this trip. It was one of the very best in our regiment. We were instructed where to meet our brigade that night. About noon we sighted a one room log cabin in a small open piece of ground with a low rail fence surrounding it. We galloped up, and I jumped my horse over the fence and one or two others did the same. Someone shut the door, and we heard them moving around inside. We left our horses and rushed the door with Ike Ulry and I almost falling in. I first say only an old Dutch lady that could hardly speak enough English to be understood. She said, "Dare, ish no von here." (Translation: Dear, no one is here) I looked up and saw a foot disappear in the loft. Ike Ulry and I both started up some wooden pegs in the wall, but he, being next to the wall, pushed me off. He found a young lady up there. She could talk very well. He ordered her down. I asked the old lady if she had any bread. She said yes and told me that I could have anything. Then I asked for mild and the young girl got it for us. Boy, that was good tasting for sure!.. Then I asked the old women if she could tell us how to go to a store. She told us that she would show us and started to run ahead of us. I immediately stopped her and told her to just tell us. Then while pointing to a turn in the road she stated, "You go dish way den you go dish way and dare is de creek den you dish way den you go dish way and dare ish de store." I asked how far was it from where we were. We were told that it was about 4 miles. I thanked her and started with Lt. Flenner by my side. He was laughing. He asked if we can get there. I assured him that we would get there. I understood her to say, "we take a right-hand road first then left, cross the creek then go right again then left, and there it was." We then both laughed and continued with our trip.

At the first turn, I saw a Fed coming in full uniform. Lt. Flenner did not notice him. As we turned, I halted him with a navie in my hand and ordered him to come to us. H was walking. After we questioned him quite a lot, he told us how to go. As he gave us a straight answer, we believed him to be true with his answers. Lt. Flenner looked at me. I knew by his looks that he did not know how to dispose of him. He was unarmed and afoot, so we could not very well take him with us. So, I asked him if he would just go home and stay there if we let him go. He immediately said yes. I insured him that to remember that there are lots of Confederates in this county now. Flenner thanked me for what my decision but he would not report it to Shelby.

We soon got to the store and went through it for what we found that we needed but took nothing else. I got a sack, put two pairs of boots, some goods for underclothes, shirts, and pants in it. I also had four or five hats in my hand. As I was getting on my horse, I saw a company of soldiers coming about 100 yards away. I told Flenner. He told me to find out who they are. So, I put my sack and hats on the gatepost and rode out in view of them and asked who they were. Confederates was their answer and they asked who I was too. I told them Confederate and asked them to meet me half way. Their captain and I started towards each other with our navies in our hands. In a few seconds, I had recognized him as one of Shank's captain. I told the captain to come on down the street. He also recognized me and ordered his me to continue. We rode back talking with each other. When I got back, Flenner and the other men were waiting for me, so I got my sack and hats and struck back for camp. I gave some of my friends what I had that Ikie and I did not need.

The next day we passed through Linn and started toward Jefferson City. When we were near Loose Creek, Colonel shanks took our regiment, his regiment, and two guns of Battalion and started for Osage Bridge. We stopped in Loose Creek then two stores and a few houses. We found corn and oats in a stack nearby. We camped along the rail fence on both sides and got water from wells b the houses. Major Cravens came by our mess and said, "Colonel, send a man or two with me so I can go to this store pointing to one of them and see if we can find something to eat." He had one of his men with him. Major Gordon said, "I'll go with you. Come, Dick, you can be my guard." When we got there the two majors went in and left us two men to guard the door. They locked the door. I got tired standing at the door, so I went around to the side porch. There were five or six barrels and a big box all nailed up. I saw an ax a few feet away, got it, and hit one barrel head. It was full of eggs. Then I hit the box; it was the same. I soon swallowed two or three then began to look for something to carry them to camp. I saw a pile of sacks just inside of a window. I tried to raise the window, but there was a stick above, so I could only get my fingers under it. But I pulled out two sacks and a pair of yarn mitts. I got all the eggs that I could carry in the sack then knocked on the window to attract Major Gordon. He came to the window and told me that there was nothing to eat. I told him to get a bucket; there were bushels of eggs which I found. I told him that I had sacks that I could carry, but that was all. He got a bucket, and Major Cravens followed suit. We went to camp and I told the men of the regiment what I found. I then went across the street to a house and borrowed a wash boiler. I told the lady that we'll be gone in the morning, but her boiler will be at our fire. The commissary found a nice fat heifer, killed it, and we feasted.

About midnight we were ordered to mount. My mule was gone. Probably someone had taken the rail he was tied to for the fire. I knew that would fall in line as we started. Soon some in the back of our mess yelled that he had found my mule. Soon everyone was yelling the same thing. I took my stand, and he came. I soon had my saddle and pack on and got in front beside Colonel Gordon.

It was dark but on we went with Shanks in front. Finally, Colonel Shanks stopped us and said, "Gordon, go this direction (pointing). Go down the bluff across a corn field to the river bank, run down the bank to a bridge and set it on fire." I had noticed some of H Company's men behind me were carrying two jugs and some cotton bats.

It was beginning to get quite light when we got to the corn field. Colonel Gordon said, "Dick, let down the fence and stand there just inside and tell the men to hurry to those willows by the river." In a minute or so, a bang from a gun was heard in the blockhouse about 150 yards away and soon several were shooting at me. I could hear the bullets hitting corn stalks around me. Soon all the men were in the field, so I hurried across, jumped off, and ran down the river with the rest under cover of the bank. One Fed on the bridge ran from the center of the bridge to the west end with 25 or 30 shoot at him, but he made it. When I got to the bridge, I noticed our men sitting down looking over the bank at the Blockhouse were not shooting, so I went to see why. I saw the Feds out in line with a white flag and guns stacked behind them. I jumped up on the bank and saw Shanks' regiment and the two guns about 100 yards of them. I ran to the blockhouse about 50 or more yards behind the Feds and between them and our regiment. In front of the blockhouse on a fire was a big 30-gallon kettle of hot coffee and some canteens with cups, frying pan of bacon fried with some bread, and sugar. I got my hands full eating and ran into the blockhouse, rolled up four blankets, got seven loaves of bread on top of blankets, a side of bacon. I went back by the fire and got a butcher knife and got another cup of coffee and filled two canteens with coffee, took the frying pan of bacon and some sugar in a cup. I then went to a bridge; it was a fire all the way across. I then met Colonels Gordon and Blackwell. They took the things out of my arms. I showed the blanket that I promised to Colonel Blackwell in Arkansas. I told him that Shanks marched off the prisoners about 70, and our regiment got an awesome breakfast.

We went back up the river and got with General Shelby near Westphalia. Near noon our regiment was ordered to Castle Rock. The Feds there ran onto a ferryboat and crossed the river before we got in shooting range.

Colonel Gordon instructed me to go to the stores and see if there was flour or bacon. I discovered some and sent some men to take the food to our regiment.

We then traveled about a mile or so, forded the river, came back to the Jefferson City road, and went north. We had heard firing of guns four miles below Castle Rock, but it had ceased and had orders to meet the Brigade about three miles north of Castle Rock. When we got there, Colonel Gordon and I did not see anyone, so we started north and without warning, a dozen or so shots were fired at us. Colonel Gordon began thinking that they were our men shouted, "What the heck are you shooting at us for?" They hollered back wanting to know who we were. We announced that we were Gordon's and Shelby's men. All of a sudden about 40 or 50 more shots and bullets started singing around us. Again, Gordon asked who they were. They gave their Captain's name as Johnson Company. Captain Wilkerson told Gordon that he knew them and to allow for them to pass. Well instead of fighting, they ran off. He then put Wilkerson Company on guard duty, and we went south of the field behind us. We then slowly marched into camp, got supper, and sent a scout to find Shelby.

Early in the morning, Shelby came up, and we started for Jefferson City. I think it was the 8th or 9th of October. There was some fighting in front but only skirmishes.

When we came out of the timber on top of a hill near to where the Central School now is, one battery was already there with Generals Price and Shelby. We were stopped there awhile. We could see the capitol and the forts around the Pen. We marched down the hill west, crossed the creek not far from where the Hospital is now, went west, and camped on a creek.

The next morning, we started west on California Road but turned toward Boonville just about night time. The next day we took Boonville with but little fighting and camped on the creek just west near the river.

My brother, Ikie, had recovered and was with Company E as a scout and had a skirmish with a squad of Feds near Boonville. They captured the bunch and brought them in camp at Boonville the night we got there. Ikie got one of their horses, a very fine sorrel, and gave it to me so I could be splendidly mounted.

The next morning Captain Elliott was ordered to Saline County and when he was getting orders at our headquarters, Colonel Gordon told me to go with them and then go home in a few days. When we got in Saline County, a few miles later a farmer told us Bingham Company of Missouri Militia had just gone by north to Glasco. We started in pursuit, but they got across the river. We turned back toward Marshall. Some got home that night, but Ikie and I stayed with William Garnert, ten miles southeast of home. We got home about 9am.

I stayed there, but Ikie traveled onto Miami the second day and was elected 2nd Lieutenant of Nixon's recruits. My Mother and sisters made us underwear, shirts, and pants. They made me a pair of grey jeans for a uniform and even a cap.

The morning of October 17, Thomas Winning and I left. We ate dinner with friends in Miami. I went all around and told all the girls goodbye, and they all kissed me goodbye and wish me well. A bunch of Company E men and us went out four miles southwest and stayed all night. Nixon's company came early and so did Company E. We got with the whole army at Grand Pass, went through Waverly and camped a few miles west.

On October 20 our Brigade drove Colonel Lightfoot's Brigade out of the Lexington fairgrounds. We captured a few horses and supplies. He stopped on a high hill west of us to give us fight, but our Battery got in a few shots. Our Regiment was ordered to charge them, but the hill was steep and under the trees so thick that we could not rush. As soon as I blew the charge, they left. When we got to the road, Slawback Battalion was in the road ahead of us.

In about a mile they were fired on by rear guards. He formed his men in time and ordered a charge, but they did not go. Colonel Gordon and I, at the head of our regiment, passed. Colonel Slawback left his men and went with us to charge them. In about a mile we were going through a lane with Company H just behind Colonel Gordon and myself. A company fired upon us just as Lt. Dolins and three of his men got in front of us. The three men were wounded. Colonel Gordon said, "Dick, throw down the fence, force Company H in there and charge them." But when we got there at the edge of the woods, they were gone. I opened a gate and we came out in the road.

All of a sudden darkness covered us like a veil. Colonel Gordon ordered me to ask for four volunteers for advance. No one volunteered then I shouted, "Come on boys! At least three come with me. I never will ask a man in this regiment to do what I am afraid to do?" Dave Poole rode up and told me that he would go. Then Harry Hammer and Dave Paine came up. We started in a run. It was so dark that we could not even see 20 feet ahead of us. Soon, about a dozen shots came at us, but we kept going. Soon a company dismounted behind a rock fence and fired at us not over 5 feet. About the first shot broke the left foreleg of my horse, and there I was in the road. The others got out in the timber. I could plainly hear the officer shoot low yet all the bullets were near the ground.

I thought if I blew a charge, it would hurry the regiment to me so I blew a charge, and they quit firing and lit out. When Colonel Gordon came, I told him my fine horse had been shot. He said, "There are several leading horses they got back there; get the first one and come on." He ordered Company E to the front. I got another horse but a poor one and soon caught up to Colonel Gordon. He said, "Dick, we are ordered back into camp; go catch Company E and order them back." I went as fast as my horse could go and, in the timber, the roads forked the ground was damp. I got off my horse, lit matches, looked close, and decided which road would be the best one for Company E to take. I then traveled as fast as I could make my horse go, and in about 2/2 mile I caught up to them and made it back to camp. We settled in for the night there.

The next day we struck their rear at the Little Blue River. Tod's Bushwhackers were in front. When he crossed and rode upon a small hill, he was shot and killed by a sharp shooter.

Our Regiment crossed soon after and formed a line south of the road and began to advance. We were stopped in a narrow land and dismounted. General Jeff Thompson took his station just behind our

Regiment. He ordered us through a cornfield. We could not see the enemy, but the bullets were hitting corn stalks all around us.

We stopped at the fence with a grass pasture before us while being a ¼ mile behind a rock fence. While waiting there, I saw six or eight Feds in a bunch. (Guess they were talking.) They were in a little cornfield a little to the north of our Regiment and nearly halfway between their lines and ours. There was no firing at that time. I said, "Boys, some of you with long range guns try that bunch." Several fired! One fell and the others ran to the rock fence. In a few minutes General Thompson walked right behind me and said, "Now Boys, over the fence and go for them." I did not wait for more. I jumped the fence and, in a run, started to the man I saw fall expecting to get a navie, but about halfway, I heard a boom, stopped, looked, and saw a shell pass over my head. In a second came another. I looked back and realized that I was the only man over the fence. I would not bounce back for fear they would laugh at me. Their two guns kept firing at me as fast as they could load. I ran to a hog wallow [8] about two feet deep, would jump down into it when I saw the smoke stand up, and wave my cap at them. Soon I heard our Battery fire. It also shot over my head, but every shot knocked a big gap in that rock fence. The Feds lit out, and our Regiment came up to me, but someone else got my man's navie.

We camped in the streets of Independence, Missouri that night.

The next morning, October 22nd, we started our Regiment just before our Battery. Colonel Gordon and I were in front with Company E just behind us. My brother, Ikie, and ten men of his Company that were armed were attached to Company E.

After noon when we had got down in the bottom east of the Big Blue River, the road turned Northwest. General Shelby was 30 or 35 feet west of the road and halted our Regiment. He then hollered, "Open ranks, Gordon, and pass the word back for Battery to pass through." So, he motioned Gordon to join him. We both rode to him.

---

8   a sheath for a blade of a sword or dagger typically made of leather or metal

The engineers with axes were passing on the opposite side of the road. Colonel Gordon asked, "Do you have to cut a road to the river?" Shelby answered, "Yes, they have to cut the trees across the road to the river and then cut the limbs off and leave them sticking back so sharp." We then had to clear the way.

Shelby also said to Gordon, "There is a wood road that crosses the river about 1 ½ or 2 miles up the river. Take your Regiment and go in this direction (Pointing), and when you strike the road and get there, cross if you can. But cross somewhere as soon as you can go out on the prairie, and when you strike the Warnal Road, turn back towards Westport, hold the position, and send for reinforcements if you need them."

Colonel Gordon turned to me and said, "You, Dick. You heard the General! Go! I want more orders, so go in a fast trot." I turned to Captain Elliot and said, "Follow me." As he passed Company G, I heard him say, "Pass the word back to keep well closed up." Just as I struck the wood road, Colonel Gordon joined me again. He told to close up and start at run. We found no one at the ford. Fifty men there could have held it against us.

Colonel Gordon and I rode across with the Regiment following. After we all got up the steep bluff and started again in a run. We got out of the timber still going Southwest and not seeing any enemy, but we still kept going in a run until we struck the Warnal Road. There behind a tall hedge fence were a lot of Feds. The first we knew of them was a boom from a 24-pound brass gun immediately in front shot at Colonel Gordon and me but only missed me a few feet. They were only about 200 yards from us.

Colonel Gordon told me, "Dick, form four Companies right into line." He called my brother, Ikie, over to him and said, "Ike, form five Companies left into line and come back to me." As soon as I had formed the four Companies, I returned back to Colonel Gordon in front of our lines. Colonel Blackwell was talking to Colonel Gordon, and Blackwell said to me, "See that draw, Dick, at the end of the line going Southwest?" I said, "Yes." He then told me, "Go order them around in that draw or hollow and come back to me." I did as I was told, when Ikie got to the Colonels, Blackwell sent him to halt the Battalion at a certain point. Then he said, "Dick, take one man a go to that high log stable get up in it, find out their position, and number of men if you can. "I took Jim Jackson of Company E and went to the stable. I was nearly to their rear but we could only see some wagons a few men riding around, but they were firing at Colonel Gordon's Battalion From the length of the line of their smoke from their guns, I said that if infantry of 400 and cavalry of 225 had gone back, I told Colonel Blackwell about this.. He requested to blow a charge and away we went. So did Colonel Gordon. Their cavalry, about 85 mostly, got away, but Colonel Gordon captured nearly 200 infantry. They left the gun but spiked it. We charged to a rock fence about 75 yards from the road. The cavalry was running south then my brother, Ikie, thought to jump his horse over the fence just ahead of me, but he only jumped on top and fell over knocking a big gap down. He then rolled off to the left, and his horse to the right. I rode through, turned, and asked Ikie if he was hurt. He told me to catch his horse. I did and gave him the bridle. He was then on his feet and had gotten his navie which he had dropped. I saw the Feds running by 75 yards away in the road. I did not look back to see where our men were but charged into their line shooting but missed, I guess until the last shot. I fired it at the driver of the casons. He had six fine horses with whip in one hand and the lines in the other while keeping up the men in front with six men with guns behind him. He dropped the whip and lines when I shot and dropped from his horse. I ran ahead of the horses and in 15 feet from the Feds. The then hit horses over their heads and said, "Whoa!" My last load was gone. I turned to where the six men were, but they had disappeared in the brush. I never knew what happened to the driver.

My brother, Ikie, came by just then and said, "Come on. Let's get more." I said, "I must load my gun first." Lieutenant Flenner and two men passed just at that time. He said, "Come on, Dick, we get more guys." I said, "As soon as I load up." Then Jim Jackson came up, and I got loaded up. We followed as fast as we could down through the timber across Indian Creek on the south, and up a small creek. About a mile or more, we heard a few shots ahead, and as we were rounding a sharp high cliff, we met Ikie and the two men coming back. He said, "Don't go round there or they will get you. They killed Flenner."

Jim Jackson and I rode up the bluff at the back of the cliff. There was the 75 or so of them formed at the top of the bluff across the road about 150 yards from us. Colonel Blackwell, with about six or eight men, came, and I called him up to see their position. He said, "You and those boys stay here. I'm going to get about 40 or 50, and we can run them out on that prairie." I told the boys to get behind trees the best they could and go shooting at them with their long-ranged guns. They returned the fire, but I saw no one fall, neither them nor my men. Ikie took two men, got Flenner's body and horse, a good mare. They left on the run.

Colonel Blackwell soon returned and said, "Come on back, Dick, they are pressing Gordon hard from the North." We left them standing there and went back. Ikie gave me the mare that he had gotten. When we got back to the battlefield, it was dark. I then saw the wagons still there, but the brass gun had been moved. I could see the flashes of the guns Northwest over a mile from us but soon stopped. I met some of our boys and asked where the Regiment was. They told me that they had gone into camp ½ mile west of me and only some skirmishes were out north.

I went to the Regiment. The black men had come and were getting corn in a field nearby for our horses. Before I got off of my horse, I said, "Colonel, do we eat tonight?" He answered, "I don't know." I said, "I'll go see." He said, "Go ahead." I found bacon, flour, sugar, and hard tack. We had for our supper and breakfast and back I went. He said, "Tell the men to get what is there and all got what they wanted." We slept holding our horses that night.

About sunup we started back North, gone several miles, and was ordered to form up west of the road. Smith Regiment was then East of the road. Soon the Feds Battery, a mile or more in front, began to fire at us. I was in the road waiting for orders from Colonel Gordon. One shell struck in front of me and rick shayed over my head. Soon one burst East of e killing one of Smith's men. Ina minute's time one about 50 feet went west. Mat Dalton, member of Company G, saw it coming and dropped his body down on his horse's neck. It hit his back bounced off some distance, his hat fell on the side of his horse next to me. His body went on the other side. I said, "There it cut his head off!" But someone said no. I only tore his coat but did not break the skin. He was able to ride his horse on south ward. Another burst in front of me, one piece falling at my horse's feet. I picked it up. I was about as big as my hand. We soon were ordered west to let Elliott's Regiment form east of the road and Smith's west with ours west of Smith. Shank's men were to be west of ours and Slayback west of Shanks. General Thompson took station back of our Regiment.

We soon were ordered to advance and soon were in it hot. We charged and drove everything in front of us back some distance. Soon we charged again. I blew the charge every time we charged, but the Feds broke every time before we got close enough to use our navies to good effect. Just after our second charge, we saw McGee's Battalion make their brilliant charge, but they charged in columns of fours up a lane with a plowed field on their east and a blue grass pasture west between them and us.

We charged soon after driving perhaps 200 yards. I looked back and saw Mark Ayres, who was carrying our flag, off his horse 50 yards back. I rode back and found his horse badly wounded. I took the flag and told him to go to the rear. I called for a volunteer to carry the flag. One of the men for Company H took it and in a short time we charged again. When we stopped, I saw two men back 75 yards off their horses, and the flag on the ground. I went back, got the flag, and asked Lt.

Colins if he had another man to carry the flag. He said, "Yes, fifty of them." That was our last charge. It was about noon then.

General Thompson ordered our Regiment and 'smiths to dismount and cross the two fences of a home. Our Regiment crossed, and General Thompson left his horse and was with us. We were ¼ mile west and ¼ mile south of the Federal Battery. McGhee had charged. We were short of ammunition, but four men were coming it, so we waited in line to get it. Ours, the only Regiment over the fences, were the farthest north of any or our troops.

I was standing by Colonel Gordon, and General Thompson was approximately a few feet in front of our ranks. There was only some sharp shooting near us then.

Captain Oliver Redd, Shelby's Chief of Staff, galloped to our horses and called out to General Thompson, "General, you need to order to retreat?" He hollered back, "I can't. I am going to take that battery with this Regiment." Captain Redd galloped to Shank's Regiment and Slayback's as well. He ordered Smith to retreat as he came by them. They all left in a hurry, but Thompson stood looking at them go.

Major John Edwards galloped up and exclaimed, "Colonel Gordon, get on your horses; you are nearly surrounded now!" Again, Thompson hollered, "I am going to take that Battery!"

But Gordon told us to get to our horses, and we did. Thompson went with us. Gordon said to me, "Let's keep the men in line as we go. You keep in front of them near me. Major Edwards stayed near me. Our men sure did fine on that run, about five miles in open field and pastures. We saw lots of Shank's and Slayback's men captured ½ mile or more in front of us, but none of our Regiment was captured except those who were shot off their horses. The man carrying our flag was killed, and Lt. Colins Carried it out to safety. It was a long run with them shooting us from both east and west and the rear, but those squads that had got in front of us got back and let us go by. It was estimated that 60 pieces of artillery were firing at us on this run. At last, we reached the rock fence on the bluff of Indian Creek, but we had been forced two miles west of where the rest of our army crossed. General Thompson, who was still near me, called out for us to turn around behind the fence and give them a parting shot. So, I turned, but he did not stop. Major Edwards, just behind Thompson, looked at me and said, "Come on, Dick, it is no place for us." He and I rode down the steep rock bluff together with bullets striking trees all around us. But they did not follow us and farther. We crossed the creek and kept going South. We finally got into a road going south. We did not know what had happened to the rest of the Confederates.

We kept going south with Colonel Gordon and General Thompson in front. Major Edwards and myself traveled next. We were just going out of the timber when I looked to see if I could see any troops. East about a mile of us, I saw an army riding south. I called to Colonel Gordon, "Look! Who are they?" He hollered back, "I don't know." While he halted the column, He added, "Dick, go to that house (it was about 50 yards from us), go upstairs to that east window, and find out who they are." Major Edwards said, "I'll go with you, Dick." We rode in the gate and asked the old man who was sitting on the porch to let us go upstairs. He said, "No, I can't give you anything." I said, well, I guess we go anyway." We left our horses. A young lady went before us and asked who we were then told us that her father was afraid of the General's order even though they were Southern. She kept talking to Major Edwards while I was looking. I soon saw our battery with their flag and soon recognized General Shelby and told Major Edwards. He said, "Yes, Fick that is them." We bid goodbye to the lady, got our horses, galloped back and told Colonel Gordon. We went through the field to them. General Shelby came to meet us, rode up to Gordon, and said, "How did you ever get out? I never expected to see you again." We fell in his line and went into camp late at night, got supper and some horse feed. I gathered dry brush after supper to make a light for Dr. Wood in order to dress the wounds of our men. He amputated the left arm of Mar Morgan of Company I. It was shattered above the elbow by a piece of shell on the last run. I don't remember how many men we had killed and wounded in the two days of fighting but quite a lot. Lieutenant Haynie and Jim Nichols of Company E were wounded in the last run, Haynie through the left side below his belt and Nichols in his left foot. Both rode their horses through the south as the ambulance was full of wounded soldiers.

We started early next norming and marched all day. But the next day, our Regiment was in advance, and General Shelby and staff just ahead of Colonel Gordon and me. Early in the afternoon, a carrier came by. Shelby asked what was up in the rear. He said that General Marmaduke wanted reinforcements. General Shelby said, "Tell General Price that I'll turn back with the old brigade."

We went back quite a ways, crossed a creek, met no one, but saw a lot of Confederates going south on the road west of us. It seems we had missed them. We turned back and fell in behind them. They us that Generals Marmaduke and Cabel had been captured and lost their guns. Shelby stopped ½ of our Regiment at the end of a lane. Colonel Gordon sent me to see if they could cross a creek south. I looked, came back, and told him it had a rock bluff we could not get down. So, I told all Captains to have their men go to the road Southwest and not try to cross the creek south.

Colonel Blackwell called me to go with him. We formed in line ¼ mile farther on. Soon the Feds came rushing at the first part of our Regiment with sabers whirling. (Gordon's men fired and then ran back of our line.). Their fire stopped them only a few minutes. Here they came at us. We gave them a round and left, but General Shelby had formed other Regiments who done as we had. They did not get close enough to use sabers so finally put them in scabbards [9] and used their guns.

I don't know how far we had done this. Our Regiment had gotten scattered through the whole division. Only about 50 with our flag was with Colonel Gordon. More of the Feds had come up until they had quite an army. It was all open prairie. We saw it was to be a pitch battle.

---

9   a bugle call sounded for mounted troops to mount and take their place in line

Colonel Gordon ordered me to form our squad on a mount behind Jackson's Brigade and he would try to get all he could of us together.

Colonel Jackman saw us there and ordered us into his line. I hold him what Colonel Gordon had told me. Her jerked out his navie and yelled, "Get into that line or I'll shoot you!" I grabbed my navie and said, "Colonel, that is a game. Two can play it, and one of my old friends of Company E said that if you shoot him then I will shoot you. If those Feds come and if you go into their line, you will be a good target." He started away and I called out to him, "I'll go with you if they start for us."

Within a few minutes they came charging at us. I rode in line by our flag and blew a charge. We met them with our navies, and they turned tail to us but not all got away. After shooting out all our loads, we turned back, driven them back over ½ mile, and rode back in line loading our guns. When about 150 yards from them, our flag was shot off the staff. It fell behind my horses. George Colins, our color bearer, asked, "Must I leave it?" I said, "No, get it: I'll stay with you." By the time he got it, and we were on our horses, we were quite a ways behind our boys. The Feds sure were shooting at us. One shot hit Colin's roll of clothes behind his saddle. I looked to see where it hit told him, and we rode on. They did not follow us. We crossed the river, camped, got something to eat, but not our horses. We left in the night, and Price ordered all our wagons burned. My good mare had broken loose, so I had to ride my old poor horse again.

We went on to Carthage without any more trouble then went into camp, got flour, beef, and corn for our horses, and left at sunup. We stopped at Nutonia, got feed for our horses, beef and meal, but before we got it, the cook was ordered out. I had not felt well all day and asked Colonel Gordon if I must go with them. He said, "No, Dick, you have been feeling so bad. Stay in camp and be sure to bring me something to eat as we come by."

In a short time, all came back. It was a false alarm. But while they were gone, I went through the camp and saw so many old soldiers. I did not go; I began to lecture them, and said, "Boys, I am ashamed of you and myself also." It is the first time I ever shirked, and so help me God it will be my last. Nearly all said the same for them. We got supper ready and they came back. When they were nearly through eating a loud **Boom Boom** could be heard. I sounded "Boots and Saddles" on the bugle. I formed the Regiment before we got orders from General Shelby. We were marched into an open field and dismounted. The artillery shot over our heads from the Feds' guns, but the 24 pound we captured did not clear the fence we were lying behind. One canister shot and struck the fence less than a foot above my head. I jumped up and called to Captain Oliver Red nearby. He stopped from firing. Soon we were ordered forward. Over the fence we went out in the open field. We were ordered to charge. I blew the charge and if the Regiments east of us that were mounted had kept up with us. We sure would have gotten those guns, but they stopped, so we were exposed to a flank fire. My but they got those guns back in a hurry, and they fell back out of range. We marched south that night to Cane Hill and the next day. That was my last battle.

We camped near Cane Hill beside of a fine orchard full of splendid apples. We stayed there two nights. We ate apples raw and roasted, and I had nearly ½ bushel in a sack when we left. We got two days rations there and had one left when we took off. When that gave out, we did without or most of the men did and horses the same. We traveled southwest into Indian Territory. My horse died about two days after we left Cane Hill. I put my saddle clothes and blankets in one ambulance. There soon was quite a company afoot with me. I got something to eat most every day as Ikie had a good horse. He was able to scout around and kill something most every day, but most of our men went hungry. Company H had a fine colt following its mother that one of the boys was riding. They killed and ate it. I saw men kill horses that gave out and cut meat our of them to cook and eat. Dave Ferrill was one of them waling and one day he saw General Price coming in his back. He told the boys to watch him. He picked up a stick, got his crooked legs out of shape, and was hobbling along. General Price stopped and said, "M dear man, get in here. One crippled like you should not walk at all." He rode with the General for several hours, got to camp, thanked the General, got out and gave a yell, and walked as straight as anyone to his camp. General Price laughed and said that was one on him.

Someone stole General Thompson's horse, and he joined our squad. He was the only one that could beat me walking. We got to be good friends while walking together. He was born and raised in Harpers Ferry and even went to school with my older brother and sisters.

We crossed the Arkansas River above Fort Gibson and then traveled up the South Canadian River, a day's march, went in camp, grazed our horses on the cane, killed hogs and cattle, and oh how we did eat although we had no salt or bread. We however jerked the lean beef, so we had something to eat as we continued. General Price sent some wagons with meat to meet us from Baggie Depot. When we got there, an old friend of Colonel Blackwell told him that if I came to his house the next day, would give me a horse. So, I started on Colonel B's helper's old mule, but I could not talk Indian nor could I find where he lived. I finally found a woman and her son. They said the party did not live near there. I was hungry and asked if I could get a bite to eat. They told me no problem and even had some corn bread, venison, and hominy. While eating, they said if they had gun caps, the boy could kill all the deer they wanted, so I gave him about 15 or 20. My how glad he was to get them. I started back to Baggy Depot and met two confederate Indians. All I could understand was trade. They were leading a nice pony, and I traded a blanket for it. I took my saddle off the mule, put it on the pony, mounted up, and rode on. They were pleased to get a good blanket and me to get the pony.

When I got into camp, the Brigade had gone on south. I slept in the Hospital tent that night and had supper with Dr. Wood. Some in the tent had smallpox, but that did not bother me. I went on next morning leading the old mule and caught up to them as they were crossing the Red River.

The next night I traveled with Joe for corn for our mess. It was in a big field and there were cows all over it. They were all colors. I thought they were cornfield beans, so I stuffed all I could inside my shirt, shelled them, and gave them to Lee, our boss cook. He put them in the pot along with a piece of beef. We sure had a good mess of soup.

We marched slowly down the Red River through the principle town, a few miles south of the river then to Fulton on the north side of the Red River in Arkansas. While there, all that did not have horses were sent to the infantry, and all guns were turned into the Brigade Headquarters and selected so each Regiment would have guns using the same ammunition. Our Regiment got first choice and had gotten Britch loading Sharps rifles [10]. There were no guns for Slayback's Regiment so they were armed with spears, and Ikie went to someone to learn to dress the Regiment. He was only gone about a week. But Shelby soon got guns for them and while here Shelby traded his ole cannon for the splendid four James Brass 3-inch rifles which was captured at Mark's Mill. We were in this camp sometime. My brother Ikie was sent to Camden first for picket duty. Afterwards he was post commander until the end of the war and went from there to Shreveport, Louisiana to surrender. I never saw him again.

We left there as I remember about first of February of 1865. We marched slowly down the Red River on the north side. One night we camped in an old field. I noticed lots of polk just up nice for greens, and we had some very strong old bacon too. I got a lot, and Lee cooked for supper. My how good it tasted! One night some of the men cut down a tree, and there a lot of young squirrels in a hold in it. They were about as big as small rats. Some were black, and some were gray. I caught one, tied a buckskin string around his neck, and gave him my cape off my overcoat for a bed. I fed him corn; he sure liked lumps of brown sugar, and we were getting some now most every week. He

---

10   Sharps rifles are a series of large-bore, single –shot, falling-block, breech-loading rifles, beginning with a design by Christian Sharps in 1848 and ceasing production in 1881. They were renowned for long-range accuracy.

soon got very tame, and ran all over me when I was on my horse. I had lots of fun with him.

AFTER THE WAR

We crossed the river and camped near Jefferson, Louisiana for a few days then went to Marshall, Texas and camped there until leaving in late March. We traveled west in slow marches to near Corsicana, Texas reaching there about the middle of April. That's where we had heard of Lee's Surrender and also of Lincoln's assassination. About that time General Thompson was removed from our Brigade, and Colonel Gordon had been notified that he was a General. He knew the war was about over; he didn't move to Brigade Headquarters. He made me his chief of staff, but we still stayed with the old Regiment. We had moved camp once or twice only a few miles and were camped about ten miles northeast of Corsicana when Major Gordon started in command of those regiments that went to surrender.

It was about June 11, 1865 When Colonel Blackwell told me to go to General Gordon and tell him that the Regiment was ready to move under Major Gordon. He sent me to General Shelby to tell him the same thing. He sent me back to the Brigade to tell Gordon who all were going with him to line up on the road going south and the ones going to surrender to line up going north. As I came back to the Regiment, I met up with them moving out. Charles Colins, our color bearer as he passed me said, "Dick, I left the flag sitting against a tree along with your bugle and your pet squirrel." When I got there all were gone including the flag, bugle, and squirrel. The camp was full of men who were left. I went to Shelby's line which were south. About 500 of us went into his line and elected him our commander while Major Edwards was our Adjutant.

My pony had died about a month before, but some of Company E's boys got me a fine-looking Texas horse that a rancher gave them. It proved to be a broken-down abandoned cowboy horse.

We moved just south of Corsicana and went into camp, and there got some wagons, our four brass guns with a lot of arms and ammunition from Tyler who hired a Mexican Freight train of wagons to haul supplies to Mexico then started south. We had gotten about 35 beef cattle all branded 'C.G.' to feed us. We also had a lot of flour.

We traveled south through Waxahachie then onto Austin. A few days before reaching Sustin, Major Edwards came to me early in the morning said, "Dick, I want you and four men to drive our beef. I give you charge of them, come to Shelby quarters; I have the other men there." When I got there, he said to take charge of the men in his quarters and go to the corral over by that house and turn out your beef, drive them slowly so they may graze where you find good grass; all are branded 'C. S." But when we got to the corral, the gate was open and all the cattle were gone. Many were in sight, so I ordered the boys to scatter through the bunches of cattle and get the ones which were branded "C.S.' We picked up about 15. A rancher came to ask what we were doing. I told him. He said don't fool about the rest. There a lot of mavericks in all the herds. He just wanted us to get the strays. He gave us the brands of what he knew and helped us to through his herd. We found some more which were branded and some strays, about 25 of them. We then mottled through the next herd. But it was hard riding, cutting out, and collecting them but my horse proved to be one of the best cow horses. But the running all day finished him, and after putting our beef cows in a corral, I got off of him at our mess. He immediately laid down and soon was dead. I put my saddle blankets, etc. in our Regiment wagon which we still had and rode with the driver.

We crossed the river, and when we got to Austin, we camped on the south bank. The next morning Colonel Blackwell met an old Santa Fe trader, an old friend. He had been hauling supplies from Mexico and had a mule wagon train. He fancied Colonel Blackwall's fine horse and told him not to take that horse to Mexico that it was not acclimated, and he would soon lose it. Colonel Blackwell asked, "What must I do?" His friend said, "I have a fine riding mule which I'll give you for it." He showed the mule to Colonel Blackwall and put the saddle on it. The Colonel rode it around and remarked, "it is a good one, but my horse is worth more than your mule." He said, "Yes, but there is another smaller mule just as good as that one. I'll give you both for the horse." Blackwell said, "It's a trade!" He soon rode the biggest mule and led the other one to our mess. I was lying down in the wagon when Colonel Blackwell said, "Here, Dick, is a mule for you just about you size." I thanked him, I then told him, "Colonel B, I don't like to accept it as a gift." Be said, "Dick, you have been a brother to me, so take it and be glad I can give it to you." We only stayed Austin about two days then traveled onto San Antonio. Before we even got to Austin, someone had let our cattle out of the corral at night, and we lost them.

We found along our road a Mexican freight train asking us to guard them. Through these we loaded them with supplies which we found in the Government Depots in all towns. Also, some stragglers that wanted to get to Mexico wanted to tag along. When we got to San Antonio, General Price, General McGruder, E Kirby Smith, and several ex-governors were with us.

We went into San Antonio just before noon and stopped in the Plaza in front of the Mingo Hotel. We were invited to dinner at the hotel with General Shelby making his quarters on the porch. We hitched our horses to the fence around the Plaza. Just across the plaza was the Alamo.

After dinner, Gil Sneling and I rode to the Alamo then over to the city. We went to a big spring and watered our mules then drank out of the spring ourselves. We then returned to the plaza and was looking for a place to tie our mules. Gil and I had been school mates. He was raised four miles southwest of my father's old house, but he had been in Williams Company from its organization in September of 1862.

We had stopped in front of the Mingo Hotel in plain sight of General Shelby about 50 feet from us. Colonel Williams came to us and put his hand on my saddle and said, "Boys, there is a band of robbers 50 mile southwest of here in the mountains. They have been robbing trains and going to and from Mexico during the whole war. The police want us to go and capture or kill them. There are about 20 of them and have a sod corral into which they drive their stolen stock. There are two Texas Rangers here going with us. Do you want to go?" We both said, yes!" He then told us, "Then you stay here. I got 25 or 30 others well-armed and that I know are good men. We will soon start and strike them at daylight. Don't tell anyone about the men I sent to you." In 10 or 15 minutes, General Shelby came to us, put a hand on my thigh and said, "Cruzen, what did Dave Williams want with you?" I said, "Nothing much General only just talking a bit." He said, "Oh, I know. I have caught on to it and am going to stop it. Those robbers are desperate men, and if you strike them, a lot you good men will get hurt. They should be killed, but it is the Texas Government's business and not ours, so I am determined you should not go."

"Now, Cruzen, there are two of our boys who are drunk in a saloon down past that corner northeast of here. The police can't anything with them. You go get them and take them to camp four miles southwest. Our wagons are there, no I trust you to take them."

I heard a shot before I got there. When we rode up in front of the saloon, a Texas Ranger behind the corner of a house stopped me and asked, "Will they shoot you?" I said, "I guess not." I rode up to the door, and Aleck Burges, Company Commissary of Elliott's Regiment came to the door with a navie in his hand. He said, "Come, Dick, have a drink with us. We are running this saloon now." Then Joe Cooper of our Battery came to the door and said, "Dick, Alex just now shot at his image in a looking glass for one of those Rangers. What do you think of that?" Then I saw that he had a saber so I said, "Where did get that?" He said, "I took it from a Ranger." I said, "Give it to me." So, he gave it to me and said, "They got my navie" By this time five or six

Rangers came from their hiding places. I gave one his sword and Joe's gun plus their horses from the Rangers, got the boys on their horses and took them to camp. Joe Copper started on a run, and I told Gil to stay with him, and I stayed with Aleck. But Aleck soon fell off his horse, and I could not get him back on. But soon a boy and an old man in an ox wagon came, and I got them to haul him back to camp.

We got a lot of flour, bacon, sugar, and coffee along with some blankets and clothing from the Government Department. Here I got a Mexican blanket and kept it until I got back home.

At camp next morning, Colonel Blackwell could not find his mule, and one other horse was gone. So, I and another man went to look for them, and Colonel B got in a wagon and went on because Shelby had broken camp. We had long ropes tied to the halters of our horses with picket pin [11] dragging. We soon found a trail the rope and pin made in the grass wet with dew. We followed it several miles, but finally we could see it no more. Then we knew someone had been driving the horse and mule but had caught the rope. We could find no trace of them farther through the chaparral.

When we got to camp that night, I asked Colonel Blackwell to take my mule, but he said no because it was too small for him. Besides he originally gave it to me, and he wanted me to keep it.

Little of interest happened until we got to Eagle Pass. We could see the mountains most all the way while some were west of our road. One night we camped on Spring River about 5 miles from the mountains. It was quite a river and one of the biggest springs I have ever seen.

At Rio Frio there was a valley north of the river but a high bluff south. No water was running in the bed of the stream but just above the crossing there was a deep hole of muddy water warm on top but cool down a foot or so. We had been riding all day without water, and it was about night. We rode into the pool; the horses drank and so did the

---

11   used to stake down a horse temporarily while on picket-duty or grazing. It measures 11 ½" long with an iron figure 8 loop that swivels (part of this loop snapped off, which is why it was discarded)

men. We also camped on the south bank. We got to Eagle Pass about the last day of June. We camped on the north bank of Rio Grande. Our four brass guns were put into position in an open space pointed over the river. There were several thousand Mexican soldiers in Piedras Negras [12] across the river. A flat boat with a rope stretched across was the ferry.

General Shelby appointed a committee to sell our guns, etc. There were four governors of the States there. They soon asked General Shelby to join the liberals against the French and offered him the command of all troops in their four states. Shelby told them that if his men would stay with him as officers, he might accept.

After a lot of talk and an offer of $30,000 less than ½ the price in Europe for what we had, the commanding officer told Shelby he either take what they choose to give or the Feds would soon get it, and then they said that only could raise $8,000 and gave us a script for the balance. That was worthless to us. Late at night General Shelby informed us all in line and told us what they offered and what the officer said. Then he left it for a vote to first to sell. All voted to sell. (Now remember as a ruld we had not a dollar). Then he took a vote to join them, but nearly all voted against but said if we cross and stay a day or two days and if they treated us right, we would join them. They sent over some men and got guns, etc. and the money in silver dollars was divided $87 for each man. The next morning General Shelby told us that he expected toto the west coast and would disband us. So, we ended up being the last organized squadron of the Confederacy. He told us all, "Tomorrow we will sell our wagons, mules, and supplies to the highest bidder and divide what we got as before."

Colonel Elliott came to me that night and said, "Dick, are you going to stay with Colonel Blackwell?" I answered, "Probably not. I want to get near the coast so I can get tour of the country when I want to." He replied, "Here, I have a man from California. He has been in a Texas Regiment. He talks, reads, and writes Spanish and comes

12   a city and seat of the surrounding municipality of the same name in the Mexican state of Coahuila; across the Rio Grande from Eagle Pass

from Mazatlan. He will guide us there and be our interpreter for us if we furnish what he and his horse eats." I said, "Colonel, that sounds good to me." He then said, "See some of your friends and I'll do the same. If we can get 40, we can buy a wagon, 6 mules, and a lot of grub at our sale in the morning." So, I saw Gil Sneling and Captain Nixon as well as Luther Isom, John Isbell, and Mose Carpenter. We formed our mess that night. I also saw several others, and before we slept, we organized a company of 44 men under Colonel Elliott and another company of 20 was formed under Colonel Dorsey. The next day at the sale, both Colonels bought wagons and teams and supplies. It took about $18 of each of us to pay what we bought but then got $27 back out of our share of the sale.

The next day, I think July 4, 1865, we crossed the Rio Grande but as we came off the ferry boat, we were told that we must leave our guns under a guard in their armory but could keep our pistols. We soon scattered all over the town. Most of us proceeded into buying something to eat or drink. An old German who could talk little English walked up to Ben Rudd a few feet from me and said, "This is my horse; it has my brand." With him was a Mexican witness and the mayor. He told me to get off of my horse that he had gotten once before. I told him that I had no doubt that he had given up his horse. Jim Rudd and a lot of our old Regiment came running up to us and soon all were talking. We could not understand their Mexican nor them us. General Shelby heard us and galloped to us telling us to get on our horses. At the same time, he hollered, "We can lick them all!" We began to get in line, and we heard their bugle sound assembly at their barracks. One of the Mexican Governors who could talk to us said to General Shelby, "For God's sake, don't let your men go meet those Mexicans. I'll got turn them back, and you please get your guns and go out of town and camp." We did just that but that settled us joining the Mexicans. Colonel Elliott got passes for his 44 men and Colonel Dorsey's 20 to go anywhere we choose and carry our arms, and General Shelby got passes for the rest.

The next morning, we started for Monterey. But there was little interest on that trip; only some long dry marches without water all day. We all camped in a few miles of Monterey as the French were there. General Shelby sent a messenger to the commander, and he said to com; we were welcome. But I guess he did not notify the commander at the fort which we had to pass in 50 yards. They halted us, and the garrison sure hurried to their guns. But after a little talk to General Shelby and ex-governor Reynolds acting as interpreter, they let us go but sent an escort to the commander. We went in to camp in a corral in the Northwest of the city. The next day, Colonel Elliott got his and Dorsey's Company passes to go to Mazatlan and then the next morning left for the west. Shelby stayed a little longer. The last night in Monterey, a few of us and our interpreter went to a theater. We did not know what they said, but they acted fine. We camped at Saltile the first night and at Buena Vista the next. Several of us rode over to the old battlefield there and from the pile of stones with a cross above, there must have been lots of them killed in front of Briggs Battery. We kept going through Lasna de Paris to Durango.

I remember at one little town, we were told there was a Fandango. Our interpreter and several of us started to it but stopped to sample French wine and Brandy and soon the interpreter and I had our hands full helping the rest back to camp. At Durango the wagon road ended, so we sold our wagons and teams. Our mess bought a pack pony for $25. Durango was a nice city in a small valley and rough mountains nearly all around. We stayed there two days. I had some goods for a pair of uniform pants that I got at Marxhall, Texas for my brother, Ikie. My pants were getting well worn, so I cut out and made while at Durango. Doc Reiber, a friend, helped me. While we were making them, a Mexican tailor came in and saw us sewing on them. He offered us $2.50 a day to go to work for him, but we did not want to stop 300 miles inland.

We got ten days rations for me and corn for the stock. It was just a pack trail from the start. We soon were up in the mountains in timber,

about the first real timber we had seen in Mexico. At the summit where
we cross the divide, it was 11,000 feet and cold even if it was August.
It rained there one afternoon and hailed. The hail was several inches
deep in the ravines and froze hard that night. While descending, we
traveled down a small creek several miles. The water was generally 1 to
3 feet deep and about 15 feet wide with sheer cliffs on each side. When
we got where it poured over the brink, we turned square left and above
was smooth all colors in the cliff several hundred feet perpendicular.
We went around a semicircle; the cliff was on one side and sheer drop
on the other sometimes only 4 or 5 feet for us and the horses. Most of
the way all around, we could see the creek. We left pouring down into
a cloud 500 or more feet down. We could see it lightning and hear the
thunder, and miles west we could see tops of mountains. It was a pretty
sight. We wound back and forth down the mountain through the clouds
and could see the ranch Pedro Goucho sixteen miles away and see the
people in the street who looked like little dolls and houses like chicken
coops. We kept going down mountain until we got to Mazatlan River
and crossed it by ferry. Here our mess ran out of supplies. We arrived
into camp and got directions of the road and started. We went about
six miles and met up with the Mexican mail carriers. I asked them
the best I could the way. We soon came to the forks of the trail but I
was sure which way to go. We soon stopped to let the horses graze on
some good grass, and while we were resting a bunch of Texans came up
behind us. WE had heard of them at Durango three days ahead of us.
They had taken the wrong trail just in back of us. They went on, and
we soon followed. The stopped at a deserted ranch and like us, nothing
to eat. Some of them including myself began to look around to see if
we could find some game. We soon found cattle tracks and saw them
running through the brush as wild as deer. One ran by me and I shot
at it but did not get I; however, one of the Texans killed one. So soon
we had our supper. We traveled all the next day and got to a ranch. We
knew corn and bread might be scarce, Gil Sneling and I rode ahead and
got there before the Texans, bought corn for our horses and Tortillas

and Friholes (corn cakes and beans). We camped by the houses, and I was the interpreter for our mess. I learned more Spanish in those three days than I did all the way across Mexico.

We traveled slow the next day and camped at another ranch. Colonel Elliott caught up with us there, but we left before they did. They were only a short distance behind us. We soon came to the first French troops. They halted us. Their Colonel could talk some English, so I told him who we were and that Colonel Elliott was just behind us. He asked if the Indians bothered us in the mountains. I said no. He said, "I guess you looked too rough for them." Colonel Elliott came up while I was talking to him and showed him our passes. That night we camped by a coffee plantation. The only coffee trees I ever saw.

The next day about noon, we got to Mazatlan. Most of us went to the American Hotel. Colonel Seeley and his family reunited. He had a cotton farm in the Precidio Valley. Colonel Elliott soon went to it as his manager.

We got to Mazatlan the 18th of August. I wrote a letter home from there and sent it by Wells Fargo express. Our mess soon went to the Precidio Valley as Colonel Seeley advised. We found no one cared to hire us, so an old 49er Californian told us to put in some cotton on his land and it the weather kept good, it would be alright. We bought some cheap harnesses plus he let us have a plow I made from double trees and single trees, ax handle how handle. We went to work and planted 30 acres of cotton. We camped in the center of the old 49er's (I can't remember his name) 160-acre field. He had some fine corn and cotton. Our camp was under a big tree that was full of berries nearly as large as small cherries. Mexicans eat them so did many birds and once we saw a big fox squirrel up in the tree. John Isbell climbed up and made it jump out. Mose Carpenter and I caught and killed it, and we had squirrel soup. It was the only one I saw I Mexico.

We killed a lot of big rattlesnakes, centipedes, and huge spiders around our camp. We soon cut weeds 8 to 10 feet long and made sides for our house and covered them with corn stalks. We had to carry water ½ mile so I decided for us to dig a well. John Isbell and I dug it in one day, 10 feet deep and to my surprise it was so warm we could not drink it when it was first taken from the well but was fine after standing overnight and keeping it in the shade.

The Steamship came from San Francisco the 16th of each month and went back the 30th. We sent letters home by every steamer but found out soon it was cheaper and faster service by mail than by express. I think it was in January 1866 when Nixon sold his horse to a Mexican Captain for $100. The Liberals then were in Precidio. I went with him to deliver his horse. He was paid copper money, and it weighed nearly 100 pounds. He soon went to Mazatlan and to California. We gave him $20 for his part of the cotton.

The next month Gil Sneling and Luther Isson sold their horses and went to California as well. We game the same for their cotton. We picked it and sold it in March for $21.65 per share.

In March the French, 1500 strong with two small six-pound guns, came out to drive the Mexicans out of Precidio. The fighting commenced about three miles from Mazatlan, the Mexicans running in front shooting back and some following behind. They were fighting in the lane ½ mile from us, but there was so much dust we could not see them. They kept it up into Precidio, and the Mexicans, 4000 strong, cut them off from the river and nearly starved them out for water and feed. It was about a mile straight across from Precidio to our house. One day we heard the cannon quite brisk and soon saw the clouds of dust along the lane. One wounded man, a paymaster, and two guards were at our house. The paymaster had hung his sack of money on the corner of our house, and I began dressing the wounded man's arm. A shell exploded over our house; pieces fell near them. They lit out for the timber ½ mile away leaving the money but soon came back for it.

John Isbell had gone to Precidio just before the battle commenced to get a wagon Colonel Elliott's which he repaired. He had to stay there four days. One night the French charged towards the river, and the other way and around the bay to Mazatlan.

One day in March, an Irishman whom we called Irish Jimmie who lived near us, and myself walked to Precidion and about 75 feet ahead of us we saw the biggest snake I ever saw crossing the road. Its head was larger than both my hands and was about two feet off the ground as it was running. It must haven about 25 feet long and looked to be 8 inches in diameter. Its body was black on the back and shaded pale white underneath.

On April 16, I got four letters from home, the first I had received. They all said come home, that President Johnson had pardoned all below the General and all the old Feds told them to tell me to come except Thom Elson. E told Ikie that he would shoot me at first sight. Well, I sold my mule, saddle, etc. and also my navie to an Arkansas man that had come with us. He had joined the Mexicans at Presidio.

On the 29th of April, John Isbell hauled a load of cotton for Colonel Elliott to Mazatlan. I settled up with them and went with him. The French sent out 400 men that morning and drove the Mexicans along the road back into the mountains, so we did not see any soldiers. I bought my ticket to San Francisco, bought an oilcloth carpet bag, an Alpaca coat. I got on a ship near the night. It was anchored a mile from the dock near the entrance to the by. Al Jeffreys soon got on. I did not know he was going until I saw him coming up the ladder. There 8 or 10 other Americans who got on the boat. I did not know them. In the night, the wind changed blowing into the bay strong. The steamer swung around and began to rock. Someone hollered that we were off to California. Soon they began to get sea sick, but it did not affect me or an Irishman. We were the only ones to eat breakfast that morning; the steamer did not start until about sun up.

It was my first trip on the ocean which was 10 days total. The sea was quite rough all the way. I saw lots of whales, some very big ones. We were in sight of land most all of the time after we passed Cape St. Lucas. All along the coast of Lower California, there were not much green fields or land. However, after passing Mexico, all mountain sides were green.

We landed at San Francisco about sun down. Eight or ten of us went to the Freemont Hotel, got supper, engaged rooms, and then started to see the city. We had gotten so used to the rock of the steamer that we could not walk straight on the side walk nor did we sleep good that night. The beds would not rock us to sleep.

The next morning Jeffries and I paid our bill ($1.25) and got on a boat for Stockton. Were two days going, We then stayed in Stockton overnight. I borrowed $3.00 from Jeffries to buy a hat and then started to find Joe Kile near Mocaloma. It was 25 miles. It had rained and the ground was muddy. We traveled 13 miles and the footing got us so tired that we stopped and rested at John White's place and stayed there that night. In my letter from Father, he told me to go to Joe Kile and borrow money and come on home, and he would pay it along with interest as soon as I got home. Kile would write to his brother Joe telling him to let me have the money, and he would see that it would get paid. John White wanted one of us to work for him and offered $30 in gold per month. We told him if we could not borrow the money from Kile, one of us would come back. I had only 15 cents and owed Jeffries $3.00.

We went to Kile's place the next day and got there about 4pm. He was in Stockton having a lawsuit about 160 acres of land. I asked Mrs. Kile if we could stay that night after telling who we were and that I knew all his relatives in Missouri. She told us that we could.

We were sitting in the dining room talking to Mrs. Kile while she was getting supper and incomes Mr. Kile. He did not speak to either one of us but said, "Catherine, what do you think you're doing and what were you thinking?" She answered meekly," I Don't know." Then he hollered, "Those horrible guys beat me!" I had never heard such words from any Kile before. They were all I knew very strict church members.

Mrs. Kile introduced us to him and told him that I was from Miami, Missouri. He still kept telling me that he would go to the Supreme Court. So, he really had nothing to say to me that night. After breakfast, I went to him and asked what we owed him. He looked at me a few minutes then said, "Why are you in a hurry?" I told him that we were about out of money and that John White had offered one of us a job, and another man near me wanted one so we thought best to go back and go to work for them. He said calmly, "No, don't go until I have a chance to talk with you tomorrow. Those fellows have cut my leave, and the river will soon be flooding all my land. I must go stop that first thing. You stay here at the house." I replied, "We'll go and help you fix it." We went and fixed the break, came back and ate dinner. Then he said, "John White and I don't speak, but he is an honest good man to work for but don't work for the other; he'll beat you if possible. I have plenty of horses; you can take one tomorrow morning, and your partner can stay here. No, go see White and make your arrangements; it will cost you monthly here." I made arrangements for one of us to go and a neighbor came up and said that he would give the other one- or two-months' work.

The next morning Mr. Kile said, "George you stay with me and let our buddy go work for White." So, Jeffries went, and Kile put me to milking cows. But he had let an Irishman have his cows about 50 he furnished either pasture or feed and boarded them. Irish Pete's helped what they could get for butter. Kile did not like one of Pete's help and wanted Pete to fire him and keep me, but Pete let me out in a week and kept his Irishman. Kile then put me to work on his farm; he already had one other hand.. In ten days at the end of the month Pete's man quite him. He then begged Kile for me. Kile said, "If George wants to work for you, he can but I have work for him." Pete begged me so hard that I went to work for him, and we got along fine. Then about July 11th, Pete quit saying that he could make more money elsewhere. Kile came to me and said, "George, you're not quitting with Pete are you?" I said, "No, Mr Kile, but I believe that I should get more pay." He said, "I'll give you $35 until the first of November." So I milked all the cows then 40 of them made butter and done all the dairy work. Jeffries came to see me one Sunday, and I paid him his $3.00.

I stayed with Mr. Kile until October 28th. He paid me in gold and took me to Stockton, but he told me that if I would stay with him, he would give me 100 cows to board and with my help give me half what the butter brought, and if I did not clear $1000 a year, he would make the difference. I told him as we were going to Stockton that I had come to him to borrow money to go home, and that his brother George had told my father that he could be my security. He said, "George, I did not get a letter from my brother but have you money enough to go on? If not, I'll let you have all you want." I said, "I have enough, but thanks just the same."

I got a steamer on October 30th for Panama but had a ticket for New York. There was no one on the steamer who I knew. The sea was calm until we were crossing the gulf of Tehonte-Teck; it was very rough all that day. Once I was on Hurricane deck and the spray came over got me wet, I hurried down and one of the seamen shut the hatch.

We anchored in Panama Bay two miles from the dock and the steam lighters took off with the 900 passengers. I saw them unloading several millions of silver and gold bars.

We ate breakfast in restaurants beside the railroad tracks, got in cars, and started up the mountain. Ironically, we could walk faster than the cars traveled part of the time. We got to a fin wall at noon, but they would not let us on the steamer that was loading at the dock until after supper. So, we had to pay for an hotel room. I ate a coconut for dinner. There were men selling monkey parrot shells [13] and all kinds of things on the street. I got on the steamer before dark and soon started for New York. The sea was calm all the way. We saw so many bug porpoises and fish jumping up almost out of the water and often playing around the steamer. I had gotten acquainted with two Confederates from Virginia who had been wounded and captured and paroled during the war coming home and three Missouri men who had went to California to keep out of the Maltia, one Kentucky man, and one Ohio man. When within a few miles of Cuba, four of us were playing cards to see who should buy a dozen apples, and we noticed a lot of sailors passing us with ropes and buckets and some with axes. I asked them what was

---

13   specific kind of nuts

up. One said, "Fire!" We jumped up followed to Hurricane deck and there was smoke coming out all around two smoke stacks. They cut holes through to get at it, and then the blaze and sparks came out. They stopped the boat and started to lower small boats. I looked at Cuba. It was so close and the sea was so smooth that I said, "I can swim to that sandy beach." But in an hour or less, it seemed to be out, and we were on our way. I asked a mate how far it was to that beach. He said about four miles. I'm glad that I didn't swim to the beach.

We landed at New York on November 24ᵗʰ at day light. The eight of us went together to a restaurant and got breakfast. My, how good it was after our month on steamer food. Then we went to a barber shop, took a bath, got a shave, and had our hair trimmed. We left our underclothing in the bath room and went out on Wall Street to sell our gold. The paper quoted it at $2.55, but the first bank said they would give us $2.46, the next one told us $2.45, and so on down to $2.42, so we sold it. The steamer had brought so much in that it kept dropping. We went to a clothier. I bought two suits, a good shirt, pair of boots, and some other things. We then went to the Central New York Rail Road Depot and bought our tickets (three to St. Louis) went across the river after supper and got on the train. It had been warm all the time on the steamer but began raining in the afternoon, and it got cold to us that night. In the morning the ground was white with snow. We got to Cleveland, Ohio the next night. In the night we went south. One man left us at Columbus, three went to Cincinnati, one at St. Louis, and Boucher and I took a train north on the Missouri Rail road to near Allen near where Moberly is now. Then I took hack for Brunswick and stayed all night at Renick County, the seat of Randolph Company. We heard shooting on the street after I went to bed. It turned out that no one was hurt. The next night I got and went to bed. I was so tired that I soon fell sound asleep.

Soon I was woken up with three men standing near my bed. My pistol I had kept in my grip and not a load in it. I was never so scared in my life for a few minutes. Then the nearest one to me said, "Ain't you Dick Cruzen?" I said, "yes, who are you?" He said, "I am Ike Campbell's father and this is my son, John." I saw the other man was the hotel clerk. I had known Ike Campbell in the army and knew all of his folks, so we had a talk and they asked me if I had another pistol. I told them that it was in my grip. They said, "You better get it out and have it handy; you may need it anytime. All the boys carry them here." I loaded it up and put it under my hand.

After breakfast I started to the river. In passing a butcher shop someone called, "Hello, Dick Cruzen, how are you?" I stopped; it was one of the Malitian Company I had been in. He said, "I sure am glad to see you, Dick." I said, "Ben, will they let stay home?" He said, "Sure but keep that gun you have handy; there are a lot of robbers and thieves in the County and as yu are alone, watch going through the bottom home."

When I got to the river there was young man with a yoke of oxen and wagon on the boat. They took us over, and as I paid them, they asked where I was going. The man and wagon had gone off when I told them. They said run, get in that wagon; he goes by your home. He had been in some Missouri Militia, but I had never known him. He took me home where I arrived at noon on November 28, 1866. The next day Ikie, my brother, and I went to Miami to see my sister, Eliza, who was married and living in Miami. It was Saturday afternoon, and there were a lot of men in town. We met Dave Feril and John Steele then we started up Wahl Street to where she was boarding. In passing the saloon there was a lot of the old Militia and Thom Elson with them. All came and shook hands with me but Thom. He did not notice me, but Ikie and I both watched him and had our hands on our guns. In about a week I met him again near his home, Ikie and I together. He shook hands with me at that time and told us that he was glad to see us. About six months afterwards Al Wheeler and I were visiting several girls in Miami one Sunday afternoon. We heard a lot of shooting around the store. We all ran out in the yard and saw one man riding and one running trying to get away. The one riding ran to some deep washed gullies that he could not cross, turn back, and shot. We saw several shots about the same time from the rear of a store. The man running fell dead. It was Thom Elson. His step brother, John Burnsides, who lived just a block east came running and said, "George, they have killed Thom Elson and wounded Dock and Bill and my brother, Jim. I am afraid to go see about them. I said, "John, I'll go with you, and I'll see if anyone will hurt you." So, we went. There lay Bill with his face bleeding and not moving. We came upon a man with an empty navie marching with Jim Burnsides. I said to him to turn him over to his brother; I caught hold of Bill and helped him up. He was only slightly injured. Then the man had been drinking together and they got to shooting at him. He ran into a hotel, and they shot into the hotel. That bunch and a few others had been the habit of shooting on the streets to see if people ran for cover, but that stopped it all. Miami got to be a good busy town. My brother, Ikie, and I farmed the home place for five years.

(Author's note: I guess my nephew, Phil Stipes, has written about all the rest of the story to read, so this is all I will say for now. I have only attempted to tell what I had observed while I was in the Civil War plus what led to it and what happened afterward.)

George Richardson Cruzen

30 November 1844–8 June 1936 (Age 91)

Harpers Ferry, Jefferson, Virginia, United States

When George Richardson Cruzen was born on 30 November 1844, in Harpers Ferry, Jefferson, Virginia, United States, his father, Richard Richardson Cruzen, was 41 and his mother, Aurelia Wayne North, was 39. He married Lucinda Mildred Elder on 4 May 1871, in Ray, Missouri, United States. They were the parents of at least 1 son and 3 daughters. He lived in Warrensburg, Johnson, Missouri, United States in 1910 and Kansas City, Jackson, Missouri, United States for about 10 years. He died on 8 June 1936, at the age of 91, and was buried in Warrensburg, Johnson, Missouri, United States.

Glenda Lee Jensen (Great-great granddaughter)

Glenda Lee Jensen is a retired English teacher who attributes her imaginative and creative writing to the many family stories that her grandparents told her while she was growing up. Not only family has inspired her to write but also her former students. She also gives some credibility to her own imagination while growing up whether it is playing cowboys and Indians with her neighbors using bicycles as horses or pretending to swing through the jungles on a swing set. Glenda is currently a freelance writer who also has had two poems and two novels published.

Glenda currently resides in Mesquite, Texas along with her dog, Ricky. She is the mother of three grown children and six grandchildren who also have been an inspiration for her writing.

www.ingramcontent.com/pod-product-compliance
Lightning Source LLC
Chambersburg PA
CBHW031228120626
46545CB00003B/1040